D1403407

EA$Y MONEY

How to Generate Record Profits at Your Next Fundraising Auction Event

By Danny Hooper, BAS

Easy Money
– How to Generate Record Profits at Your Next Fundraising Auction Event

Published by:

Danny Hooper Productions Inc.
Box 78023
6655-178 ST.
Edmonton, AB
T5T 6A1

ISBN: 978-0-9936377-0-4

ISBN: eBook 978-0-9936377-1-1

Printed in Canada by
Priority Printing Ltd.

Copy Editing by Rod Chapman

Cover Design by Ken North
Interior Formatting & Illustrations by Ken North

Photo Credits: Front cover and back cover flap – Bill Cowan Photography
Back cover – Brian McLoughlin / McLoughlin Photographics
Inside photos – Danny Hooper Productions Inc.

Proof-reading by Deanna Ladret

Disclaimer: This book is presented solely for educational and entertainment purposes and as a guide only, and does not claim to be the final definitive word on any of the subjects covered. The statements made and opinions expressed are the personal observations and assessments of the author based on his own experiences and are not intended to prejudice any party. There may be errors and omissions in this guide. As such, the author does not accept any liability or responsibility for any loss or damage that may have been caused or alleged to have been caused through use of the information contained in this manual. Errors or omissions will be corrected in future editions, provided the author receives written notification of such.

DEDICATION

*The man who taught
me how to auction
— "Uncle" Wes Spencer*

This book is dedicated to my "Uncle" Wes Spencer, the man who introduced me to the world of fundraising auctioneering back in 1987.

A past president of the Auctioneers' Association of Alberta, and an amazing auctioneer in his own right, Wes has donated countless hours of his time through the years to help non-profit organizations of every scope and size raise desperately-needed funds to support their work in the community.

I have Uncle Wes to thank for the amazing career I enjoy today.

He gave me my first summer job at age fourteen (to this day I hate painting fences) and my second at age fifteen–working as a 'bull cook' in a 68-man seismic camp up on Ellesmere Island, a short distance from the North Pole. When an opportunity came five years later to open a nightclub in Edmonton with my family, it was Uncle Wes and Aunt Aileen who loaned me the money.

At this point in my life I could write a long list of people who have helped me along the way, but at the very top of that list would be Uncle Wes, my mentor, coach, and #1 cheerleader.

I am forever grateful.

CONTENTS

FOREWORD
BY DAVID FOSTER

Fundraising is not an easy task. As the founder of the David Foster Foundation, an organization that provides financial assistance to families of children needing major organ transplants, I am acutely aware of the many issues that charitable organizations face today. Undoubtedly, one of the most difficult challenges is raising enough money.

Fundraising auctions are an important component of our David Foster Foundation Miracle Galas. Working with Danny Hooper has helped us elevate the success of these auctions. Danny has been instrumental in raising millions of dollars for charities throughout North America.

I have realized that organizing a successful fundraising event is not much different than producing a major world class artist or concert event—attention to detail, creativity, planning, and preparation are the keys to consistent success. Through a lot of nominations and many more losses, I've been fortunate enough to capture 16 Grammy awards, certainly luck and timing had a lot to do with that success. It's very similar to when I'm in the studio working with

an artist trying to get the very best performance from them......
there are times that I have to encourage the artist to reach higher
than they felt they possibly could, resulting in the song sounding
so much better and ultimately more rewarding for all. This is not
unlike a great auctioneer who has the ability to react at the right
moment and encourage the auction bidder to stretch outside of his/
her comfort range.

One thing I know for certain; when the lights go down and the cur-
tain rises, you have just one shot, one chance to get it right.

This book is a valuable source of moneymaking ideas and will show
you how to "get it right" at your next fundraising auction event.
Against a backdrop of best practices utilized by the most successful
benefit auctions in North America, Danny shares countless tips,
techniques, and strategies that will set your organization on the
path to profit.

I hope you enjoy this book. It is a quick and easy read with excellent
solutions to the challenges we face in fundraising today.

David Foster

GETTING STARTED

INTRODUCTION

Few things in life smell better than a Starbucks coffee shop after a sleepless night. And no wonder I couldn't sleep—just hours before crawling into bed last night I made $350,000... in ninety seconds!

No, I didn't rob a bank, win a lottery, or hit the jackpot at a casino. And alas, the money was not mine to keep. It was raised during a Cash Appeal that I conducted at a fundraising auction event held for a non-profit organization that provides support for women undergoing breast cancer treatment.

My name is Danny Hooper and I am a professional fundraising auctioneer.

Since 1987 I have participated in thousands of charity auctions, helping raise countless millions of dollars for non-profit organizations of every scope and size.

Fundraising auctions remain one of the fastest and most efficient ways to raise money, especially in these challenging times of government cutbacks that have placed many charities in a chokehold, forcing them to find alternative means of funding their operations and initiatives. And here's the bad news; this is a crisis situation that is unlikely to change anytime soon.

So this book has been written with one objective in mind—to help your non-profit organization generate record profits at your next fundraising auction event.

I assume that your organization has conducted fundraising auctions in the past. You know how to book a suitable venue, rally volunteers, and sell tickets. Therefore, this book touches only lightly on the actual nuts and bolts of organizing a charity auction, focusing instead on tips, techniques, and tricks of the trade that will help you make more money during your next event. As for those nuts-and-bolts items, I've included some excellent resources at the end of this book.

It takes a tremendous investment of time and energy to organize an event and fill a room with guests who are there to support your cause.

But despite those efforts, each year most fundraising auctions fail to achieve their potential. And that means lost dollars for countless charities… millions of lost dollars.

My experience has shown time and again that many charity auction event organizers often grossly underestimate the "give-ability" in the room—the actual ability and willingness of the audience to spend money at the event. Take the example at the beginning of this chapter where $350,000 was raised in ninety seconds during a Cash Appeal—nobody would have guessed there was that much money in the room just waiting to be collected.

Even as I write these words I'm thinking back over the past month—$270,000 raised at another event in four minutes flat during a Cash Appeal; a 300% increase for another client from a combined Wildcard Auction and Cash Appeal.

So that is what this book is all about—giving you proven success strategies to capture a higher percentage of those dollars that are already in the room. I am happy to share these tips, techniques, and tricks of the trade that I've gathered and developed during several decades as a professional fundraising auctioneer.

It is my sincere hope that this valuable information will help your non-profit organization generate a higher return on its investment of time, energy, and resources. At the end of the day, this information will equate to significantly more money—money that you can use to continue your good work in the community.

UNDERSTANDING CAPACITY

Never try to second-guess your guests, nor their capacity to spend money at your event. Time and again people will prove you wrong. With some advance thought and proper planning, individuals can often be motivated to dig much deeper and spend far more than they planned.

But remember, different strokes for different folks. We all have different hot buttons, those emotional triggers that can shift our thinking and cause us to take a specific action, such as opening our wallets and pulling out a credit card.

It is therefore important to cast a wide net over your audience and provide a smart mix of opportunities for your guests to give. Wildcard Auctions, Triple-Chance Raffles, Super Silent Auctions, Cash Appeals—these are but a few of the profit-producers that can quickly bolster your bottom line.

Here are some points to ponder:

• Although it can generate up to 80% of your profits, only a tiny percentage of your guests will participate in the Live Auction.

• Every unsuccessful bidder in your Live and Silent auctions represents a potential, and very costly, lost opportunity.

Consider this simplified but oh-so-important example. For illustration purposes, let's assume that ten items in a Live Auction sold for $5,000 apiece, raising a total of $50,000. At every auction, the highest bidder wins the item. But what about those ten "second-high bidders," the ones who didn't win an auction item because they stopped bidding at $4,500 (assuming the auctioneer was increasing the bid by $500 increments)?

Those second-high bidders were absolutely willing to part with their $4,500, but didn't. Multiply that by ten and you see those second-high bids represent $45,000 in lost revenue!

Here is a real mind-bender. Add up all the second-high bids from the Live and Silent auctions at your last fundraising auction event and then ask yourself, "Where did all that money go?"

I bet I can tell you. Right back out the same door it came in just a few hours earlier.

So here's the deal. You need to anticipate this situation, understand that there's a lot of money at stake, and then create a solid plan for capturing more of that money while it's still in the room.

And how do you do that?

The number-one way is to stop thinking like a charity… and start thinking like a business.

THINKING LIKE A BUSINESS

The purpose of a business is to make a profit, plain and simple. No doubt your organization's intention (and plan) is to make as much profit as possible in the shortest given time.

But to generate maximum profits at an event, your organization, just like a business, needs to be aware that there are two types of activities: income-producing and non-income-producing.

The key to generating record profits lies in focusing on income-producing activities. To that end, spending more time worrying about room decorations than looking at ways to generate higher profits is not the way a businessperson would think.

Consider this. Organizing a fundraising auction event is much like working for several months to open a retail store that is only going to be open for a few hours before it closes for another entire year!

With that in mind, you want to be running a very efficient and profitable operation during that four or five-hour period.

Here are four keys to the success of any business:

 1 *A solid business plan*—As the saying goes, if

you fail to plan you're planning to fail. Create a solid business plan and execute it. This includes setting goals, creating realistic timelines, building a proper budget, filling key positions with the right people, using the best available tools, etc.

2 ► *A profit mindset*—Business thinks in terms of Return On Investment (ROI), the measure of gain received from any given investment. Organizing a successful fundraising auction event requires a tremendous investment of time, energy, and resources. Therefore, at every turn you want to be making the best possible decisions based on maximizing your ROI.

3 ► *Multiple income streams*—There are countless imaginative and entertaining ways to generate revenue at a fundraising auction event. The Live and Silent auctions may be the main attraction, but in order to increase your ROI, you'll want to choose a smart mix of extra revenue generators designed to produce as much profit as possible.

4 ► *Following best practices*—There are right and wrong ways of doing things. A successful business acknowledges best practices, those proven methods or techniques that produce consistently superior results. We will explore a wide variety of options in this book, and offer the best practices being followed at this time by the most successful fundraising auction event organizers in North America.

THE THREE E's

Here are the three E's of successful fundraising auction events: **Entertain, Engage, Extract**.

In many large cities wealthy philanthropists are inundated with invitations to attend fundraising events. Your request for people to commit their dollars and, more importantly, their valuable time to your cause, especially on a weekend, must come with the promise of an event that provides tremendous value in exchange.

So how do you do that?

Quite simply—show your guests a great time and make it easy for them to offer their support.

Entertain

A recent survey conducted by the National Auctioneers Association discovered that the primary reason 93% of respondents said they attend a charity auction is... FUN!

The fun factor at an event is created in many ways—a fabulous theme, a delicious meal, the personality of your emcee and auctioneer, exciting Live and Silent auctions, an interesting variety of other revenue-generating activities, and perhaps some featured entertainment.

Engage

It is important to think of ways to keep the audience engaged during the event. This keeps everybody focused on the mission—to raise the maximum amount of money for your organization in the shortest time possible.

Sometimes an audience is like a kindergarten class, with the emcee and auctioneer assuming the role of a teacher who must provide constant stimulation.

Unless people are engaged, their attention drifts away. Soon the room is out of control with table chatter growing louder by the minute, and in no time completely drowning out the emcee and auctioneer.

So how do you keep an audience engaged?

By focusing on the following four A's— Audio, Agenda, Activities and Auctioneer.

► *Audio*—Nothing will derail a fundraising auction faster than a poor sound system. If people can't hear what's going on, you're screwed. Control of the room is quickly lost and often impossible to regain. The end result? A disaster that could have easily been prevented had a proper sound system been rented.

Renting a quality sound system is never a cost, but rather an investment that always pays huge dividends. Powered speakers in all four corners of the room; that's the rule of thumb. An audio technician should be present during the entire event.

▶ ***Agenda***—You need to develop a well-thought-out agenda that 'flows' and provides interesting variety throughout the event. Speeches and videos need to be short and to the point. The agenda should respect the guests' time while achieving financial targets.

▶ ***Activities***—Focus on the fun factor. Choose activities that are inclusive and that encourage audience participation. All activities need to be revenue generators.

▶ ***Auctioneer***—The most important person in the room when it comes time to make the money is the auctioneer. You've worked hard to create this event. This is your Super Bowl and the auctioneer is your quarterback.

Extract

Pumpjacks (also called nodding donkeys or thirsty birds) are a common sight on the prairies. Pumpjacks are large mechanical devices used to extract oil from beneath the ground, and with their familiar see-sawing action they do just that, twenty-four hours a day.

You need to think of your emcee and auctioneer as pumpjacks who can guide your guests through a variety of activities that over the course of a few hours will extract the maximum amount of revenue for your organization.

This book is full of ideas on how to do that.

I was flabbergasted at one event when organizers wanted to shorten the time allocated for the Live Auction so that more time could be made available to watch a committee member's granddaughter tap-dance. Are you kidding me?

Once the doors to the store open, there is no time to waste on activities that do not generate revenue. And lots of it.

WHERE DOES THE MONEY COME FROM?

Numerous opportunities exist for generating revenue before, during, and following your fundraising auction event. I have categorized these multiple income streams into two main sections, ARC and STUD. The rest of this book will highlight each of these income opportunities in more detail.

ARC

These are the income opportunities that should generate the bulk of your profits.

▶ **A**uctions

▶ **R**affles

▶ **C**ash Appeals

STUD

These are the income opportunities that should generate money to offset most, if not all, of your expenses.

▶ **S**ponsorships

▶ **T**icket sales

▶ **U**nderwriters

▶ **D**onors

AUCTIONS, RAFFLES & CASH APPEALS (ARC)

CHAPTER 1
LIVE AUCTIONS

When properly planned, managed and executed, the Live Auction can generate up to 80% of the profits at your fundraising event. But many Live Auctions generate far less money than they should.

10 DEADLY SINS AND HOW TO AVOID THEM

Here are the 10 Deadly Sins that cause many Live Auctions to fall short of their potential. In this section, each of these mistakes is discussed in detail. I also present a variety of suggestions to help you avoid these costly missteps.

I.   **Unacceptable production** (sound, lighting, staging, display)

II.   **Wrong timing of the Live Auction**

III.   **Wrong items in the Live Auction**

IV.   **Wrong sequence for the Live Auction items**

V.   **Too many items in the Live Auction**

VI.   **Using an unqualified auctioneer**

VII.   **Missing revenue opportunities**

VIII. **Closing the Silent Auction at the wrong time**

IX.   **Poorly planned agenda and catalog**

X.   **Losing control of the audience**

Let's take a look at how we can easily correct each of these costly problems.

I. Unacceptable production

Production includes those items related to the presentation of the event: sound, lighting, staging, and display.

Sound—We have all attended functions that were ruined by poor sound. An audience that is unable to hear the emcee or auctioneer quickly loses interest. Once that happens, the person at the microphone loses control of the room. The volume of the table chatter escalates to the point where nothing being said from the stage is heard, and that can cost your organization thousands of dollars in lost revenue.

How do you expect to have a successful event if the audience can't hear what's going on? Quality sound is not an option; it is an absolute necessity.

Here are the five rules regarding audio:

▶ **1. Don't trust the house system.** In-ceiling speakers (typical of those found in hotel banquet rooms) are designed for background music and speeches made before an attentive, quiet audience. Rarely can these in-house systems handle a large, boisterous auction crowd, especially in a dinner setting.

▶ **2. Rent proper sound equipment.** An investment in sound is a sound investment. A small PA system will cost a few hundred dollars to rent. Large-venue systems with a technician will typically run from $1,000 upwards. Believe me, you'll make every penny of this back.

▶ **3. Use raised, free-standing, powered speakers.** Powered speakers elevated on stands and placed strategically around the room eliminate dead zones and ensure proper sound coverage for the entire audience.

24

► **4. Provide the auctioneer with a cordless, hand-held microphone.** This allows him or her to move about the stage and, if necessary, into the audience. Make sure the batteries are fresh and that there are spare batteries at the podium.

► **5. Have a bullhorn available.** This will save the day if there is a catastrophic failure of the sound system or a power outage.

Lighting—Poor lighting is another common problem. How can you expect the audience to remain attentive and interested if they cannot see the auctioneer, or what is being auctioned? And how can you expect the auctioneer to connect with the audience and spot bidders if the room is poorly lit?

The entire room, and especially the stage area, must be well-lit before the Live Auction commences. Think about this. The casinos in Las Vegas know a thing or two about making money, and they are always well-lit. Dim lighting, although nice for dinner ambience, relaxes people and makes them feel lethargic. A dark room combined with the effects of cocktails followed by a dinner with wine are hardly conducive to a productive, profitable auction.

Light settings can be returned to dinner ambience following the auction, but get the lights up nice and bright just before the auction. Let the crowd know it's showtime!

The auctioneer must now be the focal point in the room, and proper lighting will naturally direct the audience's attention to the stage. The entire stage area should be washed in flood lighting, thus ensuring the auctioneer will remain visible while moving about the stage. This is not the case with fixed spot lighting. Avoid harsh spotlights—they blind the auctioneer.

When it comes to lighting, brighter is better.

Staging—Stages are very important. They elevate the emcee and auctioneer above the crowd and improve sight lines. If your venue does not have a proper stage, consider renting a riser (a small platform that raises the auctioneer and emcee above the seated crowd). Risers are available in a variety of heights and sizes—eighteen to thirty-six inches above floor level is adequate for most situations; eight feet by twelve feet is the minimum acceptable platform area.

The auctioneer (as well as all the other speakers) will require a podium or lectern onstage, placed according to his or her preference.

Here are the four guidelines regarding podiums:

▶ **1.** The top surface of the podium should be large enough for the emcee and auctioneer to place a laptop computer or an open three-ring binder and lay it flat.

▶ **2.** The bottom edge of the podium should have a lip or raised edge to prevent binders and speaker notes from slipping off.

▶ **3.** The podium should have a shelf or ledge for holding bottled water, spare batteries, auctioneer's supplies, props, etc. Alternatively, place a small table beside the podium for these items.

▶ **4.** The podium should have a light so speaker notes are illuminated.

Display—This refers to the display of the Live Auction items. These donations are your big money-makers and deserve special attention. If Live Auction items are to be displayed on tables they should normally be near the stage, as this is where you want the audience's attention during the auction.

Alternatively, Live Auction items may be displayed elsewhere in the room. Just make sure it's an obvious location that will easily attract the attention of guests.

Whenever possible, the auctioneer will probably want the physical auction items like wine, sports memorabilia, artwork, etc. brought onstage during the auction. Make sure they're nearby once the auction begins.

Many organizers prepare elaborate and beautiful poster boards on easels or stands for each auction item. Punch your display up with props and lighting—a little merchandising goes a long way. Be creative. Think of the impact that window displays have at the shopping mall. Sell the sizzle.

In larger venues, video screens are often suspended on either side of the stage so items can be presented using a PowerPoint display. Here are my three rules about PowerPoint displays:

▶ Make sure that slides are created by someone who understands graphic design and knows what they're doing.

▶ Keep the information clear and simple. Stick to one or two good color pictures. Too many pictures means small pictures—and small pictures can't be seen across the room.

▶ Choose big, bold bullet points and avoid using too many words. Remember, what looks good on a small computer monitor in an office can look horrible to audience members sitting any distance back from the video screens. You want the audience to easily and quickly grasp the key points of the auction items.

TALKING POINTS

● Utilize every available opportunity to display and promote Live Auction items. This includes advance mail-outs or email blasts to guests, poster board displays on easels in the reception and cocktail areas, the auction program or catalog, tent cards at the guest tables, and table displays near the stage.

● Consider having banners or coroplast signs made for each auction item and hanging these at the back of the stage.

●   Remember, good graphic design is fairly
     inexpensive and well worth the effort. Generally
     speaking, it never costs more to go first-class.
     Also, don't forget that your design and printing can
     and should be donated or sponsored.

II. Wrong timing of the Live Auction

In most cases, the best time to start the Live Auction is during dinner (unless it's a buffet). Why so?

▶   Because the guests are all seated and not wandering around the Silent Auction tables, the auctioneer has their undivided attention.

▶   When people are eating there is less conversation at the tables and crowd control is much easier to maintain.

▶   Starting the Live Auction during dinner is an efficient use of time. Dispatching with all or even a portion of your Live Auction items during dinner allows more time later in the event to focus on the Silent and Super Silent Auctions and other revenue-generating activities, or to enjoy featured entertainment.

▶   Dispatching with all or most of your Live Auction during dinner gives your cashiers a head start at processing paperwork for collecting payment.

Whether your event is on a weeknight or weekend evening, it is important to respect people's time. On a weeknight, guests don't want to stay out later than necessary because of work the next day. On a Friday night, they're tired from a busy workweek and want to get home at a reasonable hour to begin their weekend.

TALKING POINTS

● Don't be fooled into thinking that the more alcohol people drink, the more they'll spend at your event. There's a fine line when serving alcohol. At a certain point most audiences lose interest (and focus) in the auction and become more interested in just talking... loudly! Crowd control is critical to the success of your auction.

● Time and again we've proven to our clients that an earlier Live Auction generates more money. I think it has to do with basic physiology. After an hour-long cocktail reception followed by a big meal with wine, people tend to fade. At one event I did, the six Live Auction items that sold during dinner raised $78,000; the other six comparable items that sold later in the evening raised a mere $26,000. As my father used to say, "Liars can figure, but figures don't lie."

HOT TIP !

What if an item in the Live Auction isn't selling for a high-enough price? Protect yourself by giving the auctioneer the authority to withdraw the item from the auction if it is not bringing fair value. A statement to this effect should be clearly printed in the auction rules in the catalog, as well as stated in the auctioneer's opening remarks.

"If the auctioneer determines the bidding does not reflect the value of the item being offered, he or she may reject all bids and withdraw the item from the sale."

29

III. Wrong items in the Live Auction

To use a fishing analogy, you wouldn't use a tiny trout fly to attract a 200-pound marlin. You have to match the bait to the fish, just as you have to try to match your auction items to your audience.

A black tie crowd at a hospital foundation gala will be interested in high-end consumables like fine wine, or a hard-to-get experience such as a private yacht charter. It's reasonable to expect that these items will bring a premium at such an event.

Likewise, a dinner for ten at a local restaurant, a trip to New York or Las Vegas, or a hundred-bottle Wine Tree might be a better choice for a typical service club auction.

Gauge your audience and be reasonable in your expectations.

Chapter Eight of this book contains a list of 400 Great Auction Items to inspire your thinking and to help you choose the best items for your audience.

I once conducted a Live Auction at an ultra-exclusive event held in a private, oceanfront mansion. The featured item in the auction was a private jet flight to an exclusive golf resort in Arizona. To our dismay, there was little interest in this auction item and it sold for far less money than expected.

The reason?

The guests were all extremely wealthy; most already had their own private jets and vacation homes in exclusive resort locations.

TALKING POINTS

 Don't second-guess your audience. They'll fool you every time. You may have the opportunity to secure a wonderful auction item, but may feel that nobody will pay an appropriate price. You can't make that call, so go ahead and add the big item—just don't overdo it on the high-end items if you feel they don't match your crowd.

● Just because a local millionaire has purchased a ticket to your event, don't be tempted to rush out and find expensive items for your auction unless there are other wealthy people in the crowd able to drive up the prices of those high-end items. If Mr. Millionaire is the only person in the room able to afford that yacht trip, chances are he's going to get it for a steal.

● So think about your Live Auction items...just don't over-think.

IV. Wrong sequence for the Live Auction items

Draw a bell curve (see page 188) and place your most expensive auction items at the top of the curve.

A common mistake is to save the best for the last. In doing this, however, you run a great risk. Suppose that three bidders are holding out for that big trip to Africa, and it is the last auction item. But once the trip is sold, what happens to the big bucks those other two bidders were prepared to spend? The auction's over and they have nothing left to buy.

By clustering your most expensive auction items around the top of the curve, the high-end bidders will still have several large items to bid on after that "marquis" item has sold.

V. Too many items in the Live Auction

As the old saying goes, "Less is more."

Between eight and twelve Live Auction items is usually plenty. More than that and it becomes difficult to maintain crowd control. Place your best donations in the Live Auction. If you have too many worthy items for your Live Auction (and that's a good problem), place the extras in the Super Silent Auction, which I'll explain on Page 114.

Remember, nobody enjoys a long, drawn-out auction. A common complaint at events is, "The auction went on way too long."

TALKING POINT

● Examine your auction list and edit, edit, edit.

VI. Using an unqualified auctioneer

Imagine that you have a terrible toothache and need a root canal. Would you go to a gynecologist to have the procedure done?

"Don't be ridiculous!" you say. "I'd go to a dentist."

But what if the gynecologist offered to do your root canal for free? What's the difference—they're both doctors, aren't they?

Of course they're both doctors, but who is the best doctor for the job? That's right, the one who specializes in root canals.

And so, you gladly pay the dentist.

Now you're planning your next fundraising auction, and you need an auctioneer. You need to know that there are people who focus full-time on benefit auctions, a highly specialized area of the auction industry. Many of these have received a special accreditation called the Benefit Auctioneer Specialist (BAS) from the National Auctioneers Association (NAA).

Benefit Auctioneer Specialists invest time and money in ongoing education, attend annual BAS Summits, and maintain valuable relationships with a powerful network of successful fundraising auctioneers across North America. This allows them to stay abreast of the latest developments, especially profit-generating ideas, trends, tips, techniques, and tricks of the trade.

A recent survey conducted by the NAA revealed that on average, BAS-certified fundraising auctioneers achieve results that are 50% greater than non-certified auctioneers. The point? If you're a rancher with cattle to sell, call a livestock specialist; if you're a property owner with real estate to sell, call a certified real estate auctioneer; if you have an expensive vehicle to sell, call someone like Barrett-Jackson, one of the world's largest auto auction specialists.

HOT TIP !
Benefit Auctioneer Specialists can be located by going to www.auctioneers.org

Each area of auctioneering, as in the medical profession, is distinctly unique from all others.

If you're really serious about generating record profits at your next fundraising auction, your choice of auctioneer is probably the single most important decision you will need to make, and is not one that should be taken lightly. However, through all the chaos and hard work of organizing and promoting an event, selecting a qualified auctioneer (one who will maximize your return on investment) is all too often a costly afterthought.

There is a huge difference between a charity auctioneer and a professional fundraising auctioneer. The first is probably your local auctioneer who specializes in livestock, auto, household, estate, or general merchandise auctions and agrees to donate his or her time to lend a hand for your fundraising auction. His or her heart is certainly in the right place, but making this choice could wind up costing your organization a small fortune.

Fundraising auctioneering is a highly specialized field—it is both an art and a science. A professional fundraising auctioneer (and there are many excellent ones, with more entering the business each year) is a specialist trained in the techniques and skills that can translate into thousands of extra dollars for your organization.

These professional fundraising auctioneers will probably charge a fee and/or commission for their services, but their skill and expertise can add amazing profits to your bottom line. And the reason these people are able to charge for their services is because they produce profits for you, meaning a certified fundraising auctioneer is not a cost, but rather, an investment.

So often I hear organizers say, "But as a non-profit organization we are looking for an auctioneer who will donate their services." To this I reply that you need to stop thinking like a charity and start thinking like a business. Benefit Auctioneer Specialists are in the business of making organizations like yours money, and in so doing provide an excellent ROI—Return On Investment.

Better Think Twice

I remember flying home from the Twenty-fifth Anniversary Gala of the David Foster Foundation in Victoria, BC, where the night before, the Live Auction and Cash Appeal had raised an incredible $2.6 million.

I remember thinking to myself, "I need to start charging a commission."

The following night I was in a church basement at a parish auction trying desperately to get $38 for six rings of garlic sausage... and having second thoughts about the whole commission thing!

Professional fundraising auctioneers offer ten major features and benefits:

1. They have a unique style of bid calling:

For many reasons, a fundraising auction requires a totally different style and approach than a general auction.

First, many of the guests at a fundraising event are not accustomed to a Live Auction. They may be intimidated by the fast pace of the auctioneer's chant, or find it difficult to follow the bid calling. The result? They don't raise their hands for fear of getting caught and paying too much for an item.

Chant and pace are critical to the success of a benefit auction. The chant of a professional fundraising auctioneer is usually very audible and easy to understand. This is not always the case with a livestock or auto auctioneer, especially to the untrained ear.

Second, to engage an audience and encourage their participation, the pace needs to be much slower than a regular auction. People need to understand what's going on, they must be able to easily follow along and, most important, they have to feel like getting involved.

And furthermore, squeezing those extra dollars out of the crowd, those dollars that flow straight to your bottom line, is an art that takes a little extra time.

Most professional auctioneers are trained to sell up to ninety lots (auction items) or more in a single hour, and that's exactly what they're accustomed to doing. That's less than a minute per lot. A good fundraising auctioneer, on the other hand, may spend up to five or ten minutes selling a single item.

2. *They each have a unique set of sales skills:*

Job number one is to maximize the revenue from the Live and Silent auction items. This is accomplished through strong sales skills. A fundraising auctioneer needs to quickly engage and hold the audience's attention, generate excitement and enthusiasm for each auction item, qualify prospective buyers, remove any potential objections, and close the sale, all on the fly and within the course of a few short minutes!

A great auctioneer is a talented salesperson, and salespeople understand that buyers all have hot buttons. Knowing what those hot buttons are and how to press them quickly is what sets the truly remarkable fundraising auctioneers apart from the crowd.

Identifying and understanding the buyers at a fundraising event is truly a study in human psychology. A Benefit Auctioneer Specialist understands the uniqueness of an audience attending a charity event.

Let's take a quick look at some examples of the different types of buyers and how they think at a charity auction.

The Deal Seeker

This person is looking for a steal and is often helpful in getting the bidding started. I'll often blow an item out to a Deal Seeker early in the auction. The crowd may gasp that this person stole a nice color television for fifty or a hundred bucks, but believe me, I now have the crowd's attention for the rest of the auction.

Mr. "Look at Me"

Often the most valuable guests at a fundraising auction, they're my personal favorites to sell to. Typically, they are successful business people who want to make a statement and are willing to spend a lot of money to do so.

I once sold the chance to be a soldier for a day at a stag night charity auction to a fellow for a whopping $22,000! His new software business was doing well, and he wanted the world to know it. I bet his wife was impressed the next morning.

The Gunslinger

Everybody likes a little spirited competition, and often two bidders can be enticed to go head to head in what boils down to nothing more than a good old-fashioned showdown at high noon. Who has the deepest pockets?

If I think I have a couple of gunslingers going head to head on an item, I'll encourage the crowd to pick sides and cheer for their favorite bidder. The excitement and pace need to build quickly. When gunslingers square off against each other, neither wants to be the first to blink.

I once sold a framed golf pin flag autographed by Mike Weir, the 2003 winner of the Masters Golf Championship, for a record price of $36,000! The two bidders were business competitors that fit the gunslinger profile to a tee, and neither wanted to let the other guy win.

At the end of the day however, the big winner was the charity.

The Genuine Philanthropist

This is somebody who really doesn't need to own another piece of artwork or jewelry, but bids because he or she is genuinely supportive of the charity and takes a personal interest in helping make the auction event a success.

Opportunities uniquely related to the cause, like a private tour of a hospital or research facility, or naming rights to a building, wing, lab, or patient room can produce excellent results. Also, valuable collectibles such as rare wines and experiential items like unique vacations work well also with this type of bidder, and they are easily encouraged to spend good money for such items. Often these bidders can be coaxed to buy an item on the suggestion that they can donate it to another charitable auction in the future.

Grandma & Grandpa

Never underestimate the value of having a couple of neat children's items such as dollhouses, fancy bicycles, or trips to Disneyland that Grandma and Grandpa can bid on for that special grandchild. You'd be surprised!

3. They provide entertainment:

An often-overlooked role of professional fundraising auctioneers is their ability to entertain the audience.

Guests often pay a big price, sometimes $100 or more, for a ticket to attend a fundraising dinner auction. Not only that, but you have asked them to commit their precious time to your cause. At the very least, they deserve an evening of great entertainment.

The auctioneer must be able to engage and hold the attention of the audience. People love to laugh, so finding an auctioneer with a great sense of humor is a real bonus. When the audience is waiting for the next funny one-liner from the auctioneer, they tend to pay closer attention. And when they're engaged and having fun, they're likely to spend more money.

If the auction isn't entertaining, the audience's attention will soon stray and control of the room will quickly be lost. There is a tremendous cost when this happens. Revenue always drops when people lose interest and tune out.

There is another important reason why humor is so important. Many charitable events support some not-so-funny causes like cancer research, women and children's emergency shelters, hospices, and addiction recovery. But even though the cause may be serious, it's usually a good thing to bring a little fun and levity to the event, and it's always a good thing to bring a smile to someone's face.

I've often said it would be easier to train a comedian to be a professional fundraising auctioneer than it would be to take a regular auctioneer and train that person to be a comedian.

Never underestimate the profit-power that an entertaining fundraising auctioneer with a great sense of humor can bring to your event… and to your bottom line.

4. They are expert consultants:

Your auctioneer should demonstrate expertise in every area of your event and be able to answer all of your questions, and there will be many. From sponsorship development to item procurement, efficient cash-out techniques to specialized computer software, he or she should have the expertise you're seeking.

Benefit Auctioneer Specialists stay abreast of developments in the rapidly evolving field of professional fundraising. There is a tight network between these professionals—information and ideas are freely exchanged on an ongoing basis.

What items make the best auction items? In what order should these items be sold? What are the best methods of generating extra revenue? These are just a few of the many frequently asked questions that a Benefit Auctioneer Specialist can easily answer.

Remember, it pays to hire a professional auctioneer who has a vested interest in your event's success. It takes a tremendous investment of time and energy to organize a successful fundraising auction. Don't get caught in a trap by refusing to hire a professional fundraising auctioneer.

So often we hear prospective clients say, "But we're a nonprofit organization and we can't afford to hire an auctioneer." The truth is, you can't afford NOT to hire a professional. Would you invest a fortune in time and money building a beautiful restaurant, and then put the first short-order cook who volunteered his or her time in charge?

It's false economics to think you're saving money by not hiring a qualified professional.

5. They have a proven track record:

Qualified fundraising auctioneers will have a long list of satisfied customers who they have served for many consecutive years. There is simply no substitute for experience and reputation. Check references and make decisions based on your findings.

6. They know the tricks of the trade:

As with any profession, there are certain tricks of the trade in the fundraising auction business. These techniques include such things as:

▶ **Wildcard Auctions**

▶ **Legacy Auctions**

▶ **Triple-Chance Raffles**

► Double-Ups

► Matching Donors

► Cash Appeals

► Walk-Away Bids

► Blind Auctions

► Dollar Roundups

► Ice Breaker Auctions

► Boy Toy Raffles

► Purse Snatches

► Dashes for Cash

► Signable Artwork

► Bidding Frenzies

These are but a few of the additional money-makers that professional fundraising auctioneers bring to the table.

Auctioneers who do not specialize in fundraising auctions are probably not familiar with these techniques and countless other exciting profit generators.

7. They never intimidate or embarrass guests:

The last thing you want is an auctioneer who is going to upset any of your guests. There's a fine line between good-hearted cajoling and what, to some people, can feel like mean-spirited intimidation. Nobody wants to feel pressured by an auctioneer into buying an auction item they don't really want, or over-paying for an auction item that they do want.

8. They add professionalism:

Once the auction is underway, the auctioneer is the face and personality of your organization and in that capacity needs to present an absolutely professional image—one that sends your guests home with a positive impression.

Everything about your auctioneer needs to convey the highest standard of professionalism, from the way he or she dresses to the tone and inflection of their voice; from their knowledge of your organization and its cause; to conveying a genuine sense of gratitude and appreciation to your guests and volunteers.

A professional fundraising auctioneer is like a great quarterback. He or she must be able to control the dynamics of the entire event, including the flow of the agenda, crowd control, and execution of the Live and Silent auctions, raffles, draws, door prizes, and so on.

A professional is always well prepared and equipped with a thorough knowledge of the items for sale, as well as the type of audience attending the event.

Professionals don't wing it.

9. They know how to handle the unexpected:

Let's not forget that there is always the unexpected to deal with—things like bidder disputes, power outages, and equipment failures. A qualified auctioneer has been there, done that. He or she knows how to handle these situations before they turn into a full-blown crisis.

10. They are your best advertising for next year's event:

Another objective of the auctioneer is to help sell tickets to next year's event. This is almost always easiest accomplished by providing your guests with outstanding value for their investment of time and money, which in turn generates positive word of mouth—your absolute best form of advertising.

In today's ultra-competitive world of fundraising, people have many choices with respect to which events they will attend and support. Make it easy for the guests at your next event to want to come back the following year. Build on today's success.

Again, there is no better advertising than positive word of mouth. Good food, an entertaining auction, and a well-run, on-time event go a long, long way to giving you a jump start on next year's fundraising auction.

TALKING POINT

Don't forget to include the date for next year's event in your auction catalog.

Value Added

At a charity golf tournament hosted by our provincial premier, one of the items in the fundraising auction was a 12-bottle case of single malt scotch, valued at $800.

This alone would have made an excellent auction item, but we were able to add considerable value to this donation by having the premier autograph each of the twelve bottles.

I then auctioned the first bottle for $1,000, and offered the remaining bottles at the established price. All eleven were immediately snapped up, generating an instant $12,000 profit for the cause.

Paying for an auctioneer

How do professional fundraising auctioneers typically charge for their services?

▶ Flat fee

▶ Commission

▶ Combination of both

There are no set fee schedules in the industry. It is illegal for auctioneers, as in many other regulated industries, to fix pricing. Individual fees vary based on a fundraising auctioneer's experience, proven track record, and demand for his or her services. Many organizers say they cannot afford to pay for a professional fundraising auctioneer. Our response to that is, "Yes you can!"

The truth is, most professional fundraising auctioneers pay for themselves. That's why many Benefit Auctioneer Specialists, myself included, have been serving some of the same clients for more than twenty years. There is no substitute for results and experience.

Here are five ways to pay for a qualified auctioneer:

1. **Bump your ticket price**—The best fundraising auctioneers are also entertainers and, as such, add great value to the event. This said, guests seldom mind or even notice a moderate increase in ticket prices from year to year.

2. **Find a sponsor**—Your table wine should be sponsored, your centerpieces should be sponsored, so why not find a sponsor for your fundraising auctioneer, the person most important to the success of your event?

3. **Expect higher profits**—In addition to providing a complete consulting service prior to the event (thereby helping you avoid pitfalls while at the same time identifying additional income opportunities) a qualified fundraising auctioneer will squeeze more money out of each Live Auction item, conduct a dynamic Cash Appeal, introduce several extra revenue generators, and do much more to add to your bottom line.

43

Professional Bid Spotters

Many organizations arrange to have "volunteer bid spotters" during the Live Auction. But beware; volunteers in this position are seldom a good choice.

One of the best investments you can make is arranging for experienced, professional bid spotters to work with your fundraising auctioneer. Their role is to assist the auctioneer by helping spot bids in a large crowd (200+). Their job also includes answering questions from bidders, clarifying bid amounts, encouraging bidders to continue bidding, and passing the names and bid numbers of successful bidders to the clerk and auctioneer.

Ultimately, the auction will come down to just two final bidders, at which point extra bids (and dollars) can often be squeezed out by professional bid spotters who cajole these last bidders, answer their questions, and handle any objections they may have.

While your auctioneer will usually remain onstage, the bid spotters work right down in the audience and mingle with the guests during the auction. The best have strong sales skills, and are themselves entertainers who add a great deal of energy and excitement to the auction.

Your auctioneer will be able to assist you in finding professional bid spotters, and will also help you determine the optimum number of bid spotters for your event.

4. Add more auction items—Adding a couple more additional items to the Live Auction than you originally planned can help offset the cost of hiring a qualified professional.

5. Have a Wildcard Auction—More on this later. Keep reading! (see page 63)

VII. Missing revenue opportunities

Because it takes so much planning and hard work to organize a fundraising event and fill a venue with guests, it only makes sense to do everything possible to generate the highest profit possible during the event. Yet time and time again we see money walk out the door at the end of the evening, money that wasn't captured.

And because an event has a start and finish, we have only a limited amount of time to capture these dollars. The time to think about how you're going to do that is not during or after, but **before** the event.

You make these decisions in advance by learning about and understanding the many ways to increase your profits.

That's what this book is all about—teaching you ways to generate extra revenue aside from the usual Live and Silent auctions and raffles.

VIII. Closing the Silent Auction at the wrong time

Never close the Silent Auction while the Live Auction is underway.

The auctioneer requires the undivided attention of the audience and should not have to compete for that attention, which happens when people are leaving their tables and rushing off to the Silent Auction area. You want everyone to focus on the Live Auction. The Silent Auction tables should be closed after the Live Auction.

You may even consider closing one or more of your Silent Auction tables or sections before dinner. This encourages guests to start bidding as soon as they arrive, rather than just standing around drinking and visiting.

Once you've started to close the Silent Auction sections (assuming you have more than one) after the Live Auction, allow no more than ten to fifteen minutes between each closing. This creates a sense of urgency with the bidders. Be sure to inform guests which section is being closed now, and which section is going to be closed next. This creates an effect we refer to as "compression."

FACT

> **Focusing people's attention on any given Silent Auction section at one time increases bidding pressure and drives prices up.**

IX. Poorly planned agenda and catalog (or printed program)

Your event needs to find a rhythm, and this happens when the agenda (the various components of the event) is well-planned.

All of the elements on the agenda should flow together seamlessly, allowing it to act like a compass that points the way to profits. But you can run into dangerous ground by having too many things going on during your event, or by being too rigid with your timeline.

I have worked countless events that had far too many speeches, raffles, Live and Silent auction items, video presentations and door-prize draws (and to make matters worse, an event chairperson who demands adherence to a minute-by-minute schedule).

Don't forget that in addition to all the business that needs to be dealt with during the event, guests need some time to just sit, relax, and visit. So plan your agenda carefully and allow time for your event to breathe.

Agenda

The agenda provides the framework and outline of your actual event; it serves as a time management tool. It is where all the components of the event are organized, making best use of the available time. The agenda also informs your guests about the flow of the event.

Typical components of an agenda may include:

► Doors Open / Guest Registration

► Cocktail Reception

► Silent Auction and Super Silent Auction Viewing

► Call to Dinner

► National Anthem

► Emcee's Welcome and Opening Remarks

► Introductions

► Speeches (Dignitaries, Greetings, Keynotes)

► Video Presentations

► Grace, Blessing, or Invocation

► Dinner Service

► Live Auction

► Cash Appeal

► Silent Auction Closing

► Super Silent Auction

► Raffles, Draws, and Door Prizes

► Closing Remarks

Other agenda items may include:

► Icebreaker Auction

► President's or Chairperson's Remarks

► Special Presentations

► Awards Presentations

► Special Acknowledgements

► Entertainment (Dancers, Comic, Magician, etc.)

TALKING POINTS

● Your agenda must flow smoothly—each event needs to find its own rhythm. Do not be overly rigid in setting your timelines. Rather, think of an elastic band when outlining the timing of the agenda. Anticipate that some elements, such as speeches, may need to stretch while others, like the Live Auction, may take less time than anticipated.

● A good emcee or auctioneer is skilled at keeping things, at least for the most part, on schedule. I'm always more concerned with making sure that the event starts and ends on time than with what happens in between.

● When planning the agenda, always give priority to income-producing activities.

Catalog (or printed program)

Your printed program is an important multi-purpose tool that should contain:

❑ Table of Contents (Inside Front Cover)

❑ Agenda for the Evening

❑ Sponsor Recognition

❑ Background Information About Your Organization, Including Contact Info

❑ Welcome Messages from Event Chair, Dignitaries

❑ Message from the Event Chair

❑ Welcome from the Auctioneer

❑ Dinner Menu (Optional)

❏ Listing of Live Auction Items and Donors

❏ Listing Of **Super** Silent Items and Donors

❏ Silent Auction Items (as an insert)

❏ Silent Auction Closing Times

❏ Information on Raffles, Draws, and Door Prizes

❏ Information on Checkout and Payment

❏ Auction Rules and Housekeeping Items

❏ Live Auction Disclaimer

❏ Listing of Committee Chairs and Key Volunteers

❏ Paid Advertising

❏ Information on How to Make Post-Event Donations

❏ Save-The-Date Info for Next Year's Event

❏ Phone Numbers for Taxi Companies

Here are the six rules for a well-designed catalog or program:

▶ **1. Size matters:** I recommend 5.5 X 8.5 inches for your catalog size, which is an 8.5 X 11-inch sheet of paper folded in half. Not only is this an efficient and economical use of paper, but the catalog fits easily into a purse or jacket pocket and takes up less space on the tables when set at each place setting.

▶ **2. Number the pages:** This will help the auctioneer guide people to the item being sold once the auction begins, and other important information as required.

▶ **3. Pay close attention to font size:** Copy must be easy to read in low-light conditions. (Typically no smaller than 11 or 12 points.)

▶ **4. Avoid the use of red ink:** Words printed in red ink tend to disappear in low-light conditions. Black ink on a white background works best.

▶ **5. Avoid long, wordy descriptions of Live Auction items:** Most people won't read them. Keep descriptions punchy and to the point.

▶ **6. Use bullet points to emphasize key information:** Include a brief description of the item followed by several bullet points—here's an example below.

Long Weekend for Two in Las Vegas

The sights and sounds of Las Vegas are enjoyed by millions of visitors every year. Stay in a glamorous hotel; eat at five-star restaurants and play at the resort's famous casinos, pools, health spas and golf courses.

- **Three nights in a junior suite at the Bellagio Hotel**
- **Two tickets to Cirque du Soleil performance of "O"**
- **Return airfare (economy class)**
- **Blackout dates: Christmas and Easter**

Donated by: Bob & Betty Brown

Stating Values

Should the value of auction items be listed in the catalog?

Not always. Listing values can sometimes create a glass ceiling—a price point in the bidder's mind that he or she will not exceed. This is because many people like to think they're getting a deal at an auction. As a rule of thumb, if the item's value is highly subjective, as with a piece of art, state the value. Doing so may help create a reference point and establish the piece's worth as considerably higher than what the bidders might have offered without this knowledge.

Regardless, it is always a good idea to let your auctioneer know the value of all items in the Live Auction.

Discuss the matter of listing values with your auctioneer prior to printing the catalog.

It's also smart to list your Silent Auction items in the catalog or, because Silent Auction donations are often being received up until the last minute, as a separate addendum inserted into the catalog or placed at each table.

Group items according to category (Sports, Home & Garden, Art, Lifestyle, Beauty, Cooking, Home Entertainment). Make it easy for your guests to locate items they're interested in bidding on.

HOT TIP !

One of the best-designed catalogs I've seen featured two Live Auction items on the top half of each page in the auction section, and a paid advertisement on the bottom half of each page. Guests were thus exposed to two ads while four Live Auction items were being sold—great value for the advertisers.

And don't forget to find a print sponsor. Perhaps a printing company will provide your catalogs at no cost in exchange for advertising in the program and the chance to be seen as a sponsor at your event. Failing this, find somebody to sponsor or underwrite the cost of all printed materials, including banners, tickets, catalogs, and forms.

X.   Losing control of the audience

There are many things that can compromise the success of your event, and losing control of the audience is near the top of that list. You can greatly reduce the risk of this problem by:

► Having a top-quality sound system

► Having proper lighting onstage and in the room

► Allowing your guests ten minutes of uninterrupted table talk after being seated for dinner and prior to the start of the official program

► Designing an agenda that is engaging and entertaining

► Being selective in your choice of emcee

► Avoiding long-winded speeches

► Keeping videos short and to the point

► Hiring a professional fundraising auctioneer

► Hiring professional bid spotters (ring men)

► Reducing the number of items in the Live Auction

HOT TIP !

Consider placing a recipe from the chef or catering company, or a discount coupon to a local business, inside your program. This encourages guests to take their programs home after the event, which increases the likelihood that they'll make a post-event donation (that's why it is also important to include a printed donation form in the program).

FINDING AUCTION ITEMS

Finding items to sell in your Live and Silent auctions isn't really that difficult. Generally speaking, experiential items and consumables produce the best results.

The challenge comes in finding the right auction items—items that will excite your guests and make them want to open their wallets.

The key is to evaluate your guest list and match the auction items to the bidders. It makes no sense to have super-premium auction items without a reasonable number of wealthy people at your event to bid on them. When I say a reasonable number, don't assume that every guest at your auction, wealthy or not, is going to bid.

Chapter Eight has a list of 400 Great Auction Items that I've either seen or sold at auctions throughout the years. Share this list at a brainstorming session with the volunteers on your Acquisition Committee and you'll be surprised at the outcome.

As for finding these items, remember that somebody knows somebody who knows somebody....

Don't be afraid to ask.

Pricey Pizza

Dr. John Di Toppa is a prominent doctor in Edmonton, and has a heart as big as Alberta. Each year he leads a team of volunteers on a medical mission to Ecuador, where they perform a wide array of procedures for the needy.

Dr. Di Toppa is also a prominent figure in Edmonton's Italian community, so it only made sense that most of the guests at his fundraising auction event, held at the Santa Maria Goretti Community Centre, were Italians.

What didn't make sense was their apparent lack of interest in the first auction item...a flight for two couples in a private Learjet to Kelowna, BC; weekend accommodations at the famed Hotel Eldorado in two private suites overlooking the marina and Okanagan Lake; rounds of golf at three of the area's premier courses; and dinner each night at a different winery.

Moments after the auction began, I knew I was in trouble and thought I was going to have a heart attack. Nobody was bidding! Finally, when the bid dropped to a mere $1,000, somebody raised a hand. It took another five minutes and a great deal of pleading to get the price up-- the item eventually sold for just $4,000, less than a third of its value.

Next auction item? A backyard wood-burning oven pizza party for ten people at the Naccarato's house...with homemade wine.

I couldn't believe it. Half the people in the room, even the nuns, raised their hands! Moments later the item sold...for a whopping $6,000!

Go figure.

WINE TREES

A Wine Tree is a large display of bottled wines, and it is a hugely popular item for Live and Silent auctions.

I had a Wine Tree constructed of plywood that we loan to our clients. It's quite simple and plans for building your own are provided on page 90.

Basically, a square base unit is set on the floor and topped with a large round piece of plywood; the second-largest base unit is then set upon that and topped with the second-largest round piece of plywood; followed by the third-largest square base unit and round piece; and so forth until all the base units and round platform pieces have been stacked. See photo on page 88.

The wooden Wine Tree is now assembled and ready to be stocked with up to one hundred bottles of wine or spirits. Before placing the bottles, the Wine Tree can be draped and decorated.

A Wine Tree provides an excellent opportunity for people to top up their personal wine collections, and it also provides the lucky bidder with some great solutions for corporate or personal gift-giving. Who doesn't enjoy receiving a nice bottle of wine as a gift?

> *A Word of Warning!* Of course the successful bidder doesn't get to keep the actual Wine Tree, only the bottles of wine displayed on it. Believe me, some people will try anything!

Where to Get the Wine

There are several excellent ways to stock your Wine Tree—but just remember... *no cheap wine!* Nothing will depreciate an otherwise excellent Wine Tree faster than a bottle of plonk.

You can have ninety-nine bottles of fantastic $30 wines on display along with just one $5.99 bottle of bad vino. Guess what happens? That's right, bidders will focus on that single bottle of cheap wine and equate the rest of the wines to that low-priced one, then bid far less than they should for the Wine Tree.

Maximizing the Potential

When asking people to donate bottles of wine, be specific with your request. Set a minimum value of $20 to $30—or even more.

In lieu of asking people to donate wine, take cash donations with the money earmarked specifically to buy quality wines. Use the cash donations to aggressively shop for the best deal possible. After all, you're buying

HOT TIP !
Offer to make the wine merchant a co-sponsor of the Wine Tree. The merchant receives sponsorship and advertising opportunities in return for a deep discount or pure donation of quality product.

more than eight cases of wine, and merchants will often offer steep discounts, especially in exchange for advertising and promotion at the event.

TALKING POINT

Be sure to check with local authorities regarding the legality of selling alcohol by auction

▶ I usually sell the entire collection of wine as a single item. However, I've seen Wine Trees that feature different price ranges of wines on each tier, with the less-expensive wines on the lower tiers and the higher priced wines on the upper tiers. The tiers are then sold individually in the Live or Silent auctions

▶ Homemade wine is almost never a good idea

Fanning the Flames

At a Calgary fundraiser, a $200 magnum of Italian red wine that was autographed in gold felt marker by the players on the Calgary Flames hockey team sold for a whopping $17,000.

Smartly, the bottle was displayed in a glass case that magically elevated the collectible piece to what I call "museum" or "gallery" status.

Missing the Point

I let it be known that the lovely ladies of the Extended Care Centre, most in their late eighties, had missed the point when they asked to borrow our Wine Tree for their inaugural fundraising auction.

They had stocked the tree, as we suggested, with one hundred bottles of wine, but not the good stuff. Rather, it stood fully loaded with a mish-mash of homemade wines and cheap bottles of store-bought plonk. The most expensive bottle on the tree probably cost $8.

So you can imagine everyone's astonishment when the bidding quickly rocketed past $1,000, then $2,000, then $3,000, finally settling at $4,300!

"What's going on here?" I wondered.

The successful bidder then stood up and said, "I'll pay the money, but I don't want the wine—sell it again!" Which I did, to the second-high bidder, for another $4,300. He too agreed to pay the price, but refused to take the wine.

When it quickly became evident that nobody else was going to bid on the entire Wine Tree, I asked if anyone would consider taking a single bottle for $100. Twenty people responded, raising another $2,000 for the cause.

At that point, I auctioned the remaining eighty bottles for an additional $1,200, raising a total of $11,800 from a Wine Tree that had about $600 worth of wine on it.

Needless to say, the ladies in their eighties were quite smug.

CONSIGNMENT ITEMS

Some companies are in the business of supplying extraordinary auction packages to non-profit organizations planning fundraising events. The most popular of these packages involve elaborate experiential items such as camel rides across the Sahara; center-line seats at the Super Bowl; shopping sprees to Nordstrom in New York; VIP passes at the Masters golf tournament in Augusta—the sort of stuff you'd have a hard time putting together on your own.

But here's the catch. These items come with a price tag, one that guarantees the company providing the auction packages (the consignor) a specified amount of money if, and only if, the item is sold.

Your organization makes its money on the spread—the difference between the guaranteed price (minimum bid), and the selling price.

As with most choices in life, there are pros and cons to consider.

Pros

1 ▶ Consignment items can create excitement and get people buzzing. The right items can even help attract people to your event.

2 ▶ There is no risk. Payment to the consignment company is always made after the item has sold. If an item fails to achieve the reserve bid it doesn't sell, and you're off the hook.

3 ▶ If an item does sell at an attractive price, one that provides your organization with a handsome profit, the item can be offered multiple times. Let's say the minimum bid on a consignment item is $3,500 and it sells for $7,500 at your event. You just made a $4,000 profit. The auctioneer is then able to offer another identical package to the second-high bidder for the matching price of $7,500. If accepted, your profit just doubled from $4,000 to $8,000. In a blink.

4 ▶ A couple of exciting consignment items secured early in the acquisition process can set the bar high and help attract other high-quality donations.

Cons

1 ▷ If a consignment item that has a minimum bid of $3,500 sells for just $4,000, your organization only makes a spread of $500. That's not much of a profit, considering that $4,000 worth of buying power was just sucked out of your room. That money, had it been spent on a non-consignment item, would have gone straight to your bottom line.

2▷ Some event organizers get lazy and rely too heavily on consignment items. There is great risk in this, especially if the items are not properly matched to your audience. I've personally had the horrible experience of not being able to sell six of eight consignment items in a ten-lot Live Auction. Now that's embarrassing!

3▷ Don't overload on the consignment items. I recommend that no more than 20% of your Live Auction and 10% of your Silent Auction should be consignments, unless underwritten.

4▷ Consignment items have their place, but they are not always necessary, nor are they always a good idea. And they're no substitute for the effort it takes to go find excellent auction items that are pure donations... and pure profit.

5▷ A consignment item can sometimes be used as a loss leader, meaning that a particular item, though not expected to generate a large profit, may still be valuable in attracting people to your event.

6▷ Don't forget about underwriters, which I'll talk about in Chapter Six. Find somebody to pay the guaranteed price on a consignment item—that person then becomes the donor of the exquisite item, and every penny it sells for is pure profit.

7▷ When choosing consignment items, be selective. Look for items that you can realistically expect to sell for at least double the minimum bid.

TALKING POINT

Though many organizations tell us they can't afford to hire a professional fundraising auctioneer, an investment that almost always adds several thousand dollars to their bottom line, they have no problem...

agreeing to pay as much money, or more, for a consignment item that might only produce a profit of $500.

I don't get it.

THE DOUBLE-UP

This is the fastest and easiest way to drive extra profits straight to your bottom line during the Live Auction. It involves selling a particular Live Auction item multiple times.

How it works:

The auctioneer sells a Live Auction item, say a dinner for eight with fine wine at a local restaurant, for $2,000.

The second-high bidder stopped bidding at $1,900.

As soon as the auctioneer says "Sold!" he or she turns to the second-high bidder and offers a second, identical package if that bidder will match the winning bidder's price of $2,000. Most of the time, the second bidder will accept the offer.

The package has now sold twice, generating double the profit. Hence the term Double-Up.

But what now? We only have the one donation from the restaurant!

At the time the initial donation was solicited, the following ask should have been made of the restaurant owner: "If your dinner package sells for a nice high price, say $X or more, would you consider donating a second, identical package?"

Reasons the restaurant owner may say YES:

▶ The donation selling for a high price at the event is good promotion for the restaurant and validates it as a good place to eat. Guests in the audience may add that particular restaurant to their must-try list.

▶ Donating a second package is a potential opportunity for the owner to introduce new customers to his or her restaurant.

▶ This is an opportunity for the restaurant owner to make an even more generous donation to your non-profit organization, thereby increasing goodwill for his or her restaurant.

If the restaurant owner says NO:

▶ Offer to pay the owner's hard cost on the second package. For example, the full menu cost of dinner and wine may be $100 per person, or $800 for the group of eight, but the hard cost to the restaurateur may be 40% of menu pricing, or $320. You would offer to pay $320 for the second package.

▶ By selling a second package at $2,000 and subtracting the $320 in hard costs, you still pocket a profit of $1,680.

If the restaurant owner still says NO:

▶ Sell the second package anyway. Pay the full menu cost ($800) to the restaurant. You still realize a net profit of $1,200.

▶ Here's a great idea. Find somebody to underwrite the cost of the second dinner. This can actually be done after the auction event but prior to the dinner at the restaurant.

Example: "Mr. Smith, we sold a second dinner for eight at our auction because another bidder offered $2,000. But this second dinner was not donated by the restaurant, and it will cost us $800. We know that you're a great supporter of our charity and we were wondering if you would consider underwriting the cost of this second dinner as a donation to our organization?"

It never hurts to ask.

HOT TIP !

It may be possible to offer Mr. Smith a charitable tax receipt for this donation. Check with your accountant.

TALKING POINTS

● It is always a good idea to have the discussion about Doubling-Up with all donors at the time of procurement.

● One of the clear advantages of dealing with auction consignment companies is that most will automatically allow the auctioneer to Double-Up at his or her discretion if the organizer is satisfied with the profit being achieved.

● Doubling-Up typically works best with experiential items such as restaurant packages, dinner parties, pig roasts, helicopter rides, and so on. Obviously, if the item is a vacation timeshare donated for a specific date, it most likely cannot be Doubled-Up. Same goes for a piece of original art.

The Kiss of Death

One of the worst things you can do is have a trip in the Live Auction that is ONLY good on a specified date (e.g. April 12-19). Most people at the event will have no idea if their schedules are free on that given date, and this uncertainty will prohibit them from bidding on the item.

CHAPTER 2
SPECIALTY AND NOVELTY AUCTIONS

WILDCARD AUCTION™

The Wildcard Auction is an idea I came up with several years ago in response to an overlooked opportunity. Often at the end of an auction event somebody will approach me and say, "I would have been happy to donate something to the Live Auction, but nobody asked." After hearing this over and over through the years, I came up with a simple but highly profitable idea.

Why not ask for donations of Live Auction items at the event?

At my next auction, I tossed a pair of neon-colored index cards on each table and invited guests to make on-the-spot donations by writing their name, phone number, and a description of their Wildcard Auction item on one of the cards.

To say the least, the results were overwhelming!

The first time I tried the Wildcard Auction idea it raised a whopping $46,500. One guest donated a pig roast for twenty people; another donated a luxury suite for twelve people to enjoy an NHL hockey game in our city.

I created much fanfare as these items came forward and with the excitement building, donations just kept rolling in.

It was fun and exciting. And best of all, every single dollar raised from the Wildcard Auction was 'found money' that the Rotarians didn't even have to work for.

How it works:

❑ Place two neon-colored index cards on each table. Over the years I've tried a variety of cards (plain white, custom-printed, etc.) but find that nothing works better than the simple neon ones—bright and easy to see, inexpensive, and readily available at most office supply stores. I like the 3" X 5" Oxford 90145 Ruled Index Cards – Glow Assorted.

❑ At the beginning of the event, the emcee or auctioneer explains to the audience that donations to the Wildcard Auction would be greatly appreciated, and then proceeds to solicit donations. It's a good idea to plant the seed by giving guests concrete ideas of what constitutes a great donation—concert tickets; a timeshare at a vacation property; a new air-conditioning unit installed in your home, etc. You want substantial items of high value, not a $15 haircut from the local barber.

❑ Instruct guests to write a detailed description of their donation on the card, along with their name and phone number.

❑ When a donation card is brought forward, confirm that the donor name, phone number, and detailed description of the item are legible. The emcee or auctioneer should acknowledge the donation and recognize the donor as soon as possible. This builds excitement and encourages others to donate.

❑ The donation is recorded by a volunteer who also later records the name and contact information of the buyer. This can be done in several ways. The buyer information can be recorded on the back of the neon card, or on a separate sheet designed ahead of time to track the Wildcard Auction donors and buyers. If guests have pre-registered and are using Bid Card numbers, the process can be as simple as recording the buyer's Bid Card number and the sale price on the neon index card once the item has been auctioned, then taking it straight to the cashier for inputting.

We use a custom-printed four-copy form with the donor, buyer, cashier, and auctioneer each receiving a copy. For a sample copy of the form we use, see the Resources section (see page 189).

Here's a sample script for your emcee or auctioneer:

❝ Ladies and gentleman, we have a bit of a problem here this evening and we need your help. With only X number of items in tonight's Live Auction, we may fall short of our goal, and so we're going to have what we call a Wildcard Auction. I'd like to ask if there's anybody here who will consider donating an auction item? ❞

❝ I often have people come up at the end of an auction and tell me they would have donated something had they been asked. Well, I'm asking you now. If you'd like to make a donation,

A $3,600 Snip Snip

The local doctor in the town of Cold Lake, Alberta, made an interesting Wildcard Auction donation at a fundraising event in support of STARS, the provincial air ambulance helicopter service.

The donation, a painless vasectomy for two (I thought that's how they come) fetched $3,600 from a gentleman whose wife jumped up and shouted for joy when I said, "Sold!"

And I could see why. She was eight months pregnant.

please take the neon-colored card on your table and write down your name, phone number, and a description of your donation. Then bring the card up to me. **"**

" Perhaps you have season tickets for a local sport team, for the symphony, or for an upcoming concert—would you consider donating a pair of tickets for one night? Maybe you own a vacation property or a timeshare that you could offer? Are you a good cook— maybe you could host cooking lessons and a nice dinner with wine? **"**

" Just fill out the neon card at your table and bring it up! **"**

Priming the Pump

If you're planning to do a Wildcard Auction as part of your event (and why wouldn't you?) it's a great idea to "prime the pump." That means arranging ahead of time for somebody to make a donation shortly after the emcee or auctioneer announces the Wildcard Auction.

Maybe you've had a last-minute donation come in that could be treated as a Wildcard Auction. Perhaps you know someone who will be attending your fundraiser that has season tickets to a sporting event. Tell them about the Wildcard Auction and ask if they'd agree to prime the pump by being the first to step up with a donation.

It is important to recognize donors as soon as possible. Acknowledging the first donations and applauding the donors builds excitement and awareness for the Wildcard Auction, which in turn encourages others to participate.

A sporting goods rep at one of my auctions donated a complete head-to-toe set of hockey equipment that sold for a great price in the Wildcard Auction. He was so pleased with the impromptu exposure it gave his company that he offered to sponsor the next year's event and make another donation of hockey equipment to the following year's Live Auction.

Not knowing what's going to be donated adds an element of surprise and entertainment. You'll see some pretty crazy donations come forward—things you'd never think to ask for.

HOT TIP !
The Wildcard Auction helps identify prospective donors and sponsors for future events.

Features and Benefits of the Wildcard Auction

▶ Fast and easy to execute

▶ Casts a wide net over the audience, often capturing donations from folks you'd never think of asking

▶ Adds "found money" directly to your bottom line

▶ Requires little to no work ahead of time

▶ Helps identify future donors and sponsors for your event

▶ It's entertaining, engaging, and extracts extra revenue

There is one caveat: The Wildcard Auction doesn't always work. Sometimes nobody makes a donation. But other times it works like magic, adding thousands of extra dollars directly to your bottom line. One thing is certain; you won't know unless you try. What do you have to lose?

Sample Wildcard Auction items that I've sold:

▶ Pig roasts for twenty and forty people

▶ Thirty dozen homemade perogies

▶ Side of beef cut and wrapped for the freezer

▶ Tickets to sporting, theater, and concert events

▶ Professional photography session

▶ Autographed hockey jersey

▶ New furnace/air conditioner installed in a home or cottage

▶ Fine scotch tasting

▶ Ride in a helicopter/airplane

▶ Cooking lessons

▶ Complete head-to-toe set of new hockey equipment

▶ Three-day Porsche rental with accommodation and dinner at a mountain resort

▶ Seven nights at a vacation property

▶ Golf lessons

▶ Guided gopher hunt in a stolen truck with unregistered firearms and all the beer you can drink (I'm serious—this item sold for $1,000 to a local RCMP staff sergeant)

What if you receive too many Wildcard donations?

Simply choose the best donations, time permitting, and ask the remaining donors if they would consider rolling their donations forward to next year's event.

Pew With A View

At a fundraising auction being held at Our Lady of Perpetual Help Church, Father Jack Hamilton made an interesting donation to the Wildcard Auction.

He called it "A Pew With a View" —guaranteed front row seating at midnight Mass on Christmas Eve for a family of four. What a great idea... stay home and relax until quarter to twelve, then waltz right in like you own the place!

The item raised $3,000.

BLIND AUCTION

Blind Auctions are easy and entertaining, and they are a great way to raise extra money at your event. Three lucky bidders get to choose a suitcase, box, purse, or other container. Each has a prize inside… but which one holds the grand prize?

How it works:

You need three prizes—one grand prize, one good prize, and one mediocre prize. For example:

▶ A seven-night trip to Las Vegas for two

▶ A fifty-two-inch flat screen television

▶ A pizza party for ten

You'll also need three envelopes, each containing a letter that describes a prize, and three identical things in which to hide the three envelopes (inside suitcases or boxes; under cowboy hats or construction hardhats; behind three doors, etc.)

Suppose the grand prize is a trip to Las Vegas, and you're using three suitcases to conceal the envelopes. The auctioneer describes all three prizes, placing a great deal of emphasis on the big prize—the trip—then auctions off first choice of a suitcase. The highest bidder is asked to come up on stage and wait until the auctioneer sells off the second and third suitcases (three separate auctions).

Once all three suitcases have been auctioned off and the successful bidders are standing up on the stage, the auctioneer asks the first bidder to choose a suitcase. The crowd really likes to get involved here. Once a suitcase is chosen, the emcee or auctioneer opens it, retrieves the envelope, and announces the prize.

Repeat for the second and third bidders—easy, entertaining, and lots of fun!

PURSE-SNATCHER AUCTION

In the Purse-Snatcher Auction, five or six beautiful purses are individually auctioned off. Inside one of these purses is a bundle of cash. Who will be the lucky purse buyer?

How it works:

Five or six volunteers each take a new purse and walk through the audience. Guests are invited to place a cash donation in a purse. Once the cash has all been collected and counted, the entire amount is secretly hidden inside one of the purses.

The auctioneer then sells the purses individually. The purses remain onstage until all the purses have been auctioned, at which time the successful bidders each come to the stage and claim the purse they purchased.

Bidders are not allowed to look inside their purse until instructed to do so by the auctioneer.

The bidder whose purse holds the cash is declared the purse-snatcher.

In lieu of collecting cash and hiding it in a purse, you could place a certificate redeemable for a grand prize. Obviously, the grander the prize, the more the purses will sell for.

HOT-POTATO AUCTION

In the Hot-Potato Auction, an item is auctioned off and then immediately donated back by the successful bidder to be re-auctioned.

How it works:

At one of my auction events a decorated cake that looked like a beautiful teapot was donated. It sold for $800. The successful bidder kindly donated the cake to be sold again. At this point, I suggested that it would be fun to see how many people would buy this cake and then donate it back. The cake ended up selling numerous times, each time for a different amount. In total, it raised more than $4,000 for the charity!

CENTERPIECE AUCTION

In the Centerpiece Auction, a guest acts as the auctioneer and auctions off the centerpiece at his/her table.

How it works:

One guest at each table volunteers (or is volunteered) as the centerpiece auctioneer.

Following the instructions of the real auctioneer, the centerpiece auctioneers are asked to stand. A prize is offered for the volunteer auctioneer who raises the most amount of money for his or her centerpiece. There is a two-minute time limit for each table.

At the end of two minutes, the winning centerpiece auctioneer is declared and comes forward to receive the prize while volunteers visit each table to record the name and Bid Card number of each successful centerpiece bidder, who then pays for their centerpiece purchase right away, or at the end of the event.

The first time I tried this idea was at a large fundraising event in support of a young lady fighting cancer. Five of the volunteer auctioneers raised their hands when I asked if anyone had raised $1,000 or more for their centerpiece. I had them all come forward and declare their sale prices—the winner sold his centerpiece for a whopping $4,000!

71

GIFT CERTIFICATE BIDDING FRENZY

This is the best method I've seen for selling gift certificates at full, or higher than, face value.

How it works:

The auctioneer has a number of gift certificates to individually sell from the main stage. Rather than auction them in the typical manner, the auctioneer takes the first gift certificate, holds it up, and asks who will pay 50% of the face value.

Example: "I have a $100 gift certificate for the Keg Steakhouse. Who would like to buy it for $50?"

Several hands go up.

"Please keep your hand raised if you'd pay $75."

Several people drop their hands.

"And who would pay $100?"

Asking people to keep their hands raised, the auctioneer asks for increasingly higher amounts. Hands drop as the bid climbs. However, more often than not, a few bidders will keep their hands raised well past the full face value of the certificate.

TALKING POINT

When gift certificates are placed in the Silent Auction, you're lucky if they generate 50% of face value. A Bidding Frenzy, on the other hand, often generates 100% to 150% of face value.

Who knows why, but this really works!

TREASURE CHEST AUCTION

The auctioneer sells a small trunk or chest filled with lotto tickets and several mystery items.

> ## TALKING POINT
>
> ❧ It's a good idea to have at least one valuable item, such as a nice piece of jewelry, that the auctioneer can confirm is inside the chest.

LEGACY AUCTION

In a Legacy Auction, an item sold in the Live Auction is given to the successful bidder to enjoy until the following year's auction, at which time it is returned to the charity organization to be resold.

How it works:

My first experience doing a Legacy Auction was at an amazing event, the Festival of Trees in Prince George, British Columbia.

One of the items on offer was a three-foot aluminum Christmas tree, originally purchased in the early 1950s at Perry's Pharmacy by Bea Dezell, the local Brownie pack leader. For many Christmases it served as the Brownie pack's tree, until eventually it was retired and stowed away in Bea's basement.

One day, many years later, the little tree appeared in a garage sale. A former Brownie, now a grown woman, recognized the tree and snapped it up at the bargain-basement price of $1.

In time the tree found its way to the Spirit of the North Healthcare Foundation Festival of Trees, where it struck an emotional chord with many of the women who remembered having adorned "Bea's Tree" with beautiful homemade decorations back in their Brownie days.

The event organizers astutely decided that Bea's Tree should be treated as a Legacy Auction item, meaning that whoever bought it at the Festival of Trees would have the right to enjoy the tree for the holidays, after which it would be returned to be sold again the following year.

Between 2004 and 2012 that little aluminum Christmas tree, once

It Worked For The Zoo Too

On a much grander scale, the Calgary Zoo for several years enjoyed great success with its Legacy Auction. A series of life-size wood animal carvings were auctioned each year, the idea being that the corporations or individuals purchasing these spectacular pieces of art would have them to enjoy and display for a period of three years before returning them to be resold.

A new series of carvings was introduced each year and added to the rotation. Several of these life-like pieces sold for tens of thousands of dollars, and I couldn't begin to speculate how much money was generated over the years by this brilliant idea.

orphaned until being rediscovered in a garage sale, raised a jaw-dropping $93,650 for the foundation.

Talk about a return on investment!

CHAPTER 3
SILENT AUCTIONS

A Silent Auction is a simple, fun, and profitable way to merchandize numerous items at the same time. It is similar to the Live Auction in that items are sold to the highest bidder. The difference is that all items are displayed on tables and available to bid on right at the start of your fundraising event. There is no auctioneer calling for bids (hence the term Silent Auction).

The purpose of the Silent Auction is to provide your guests with an entertaining opportunity to purchase a few great items (an ideal ratio is one to 1.5 items per couple) at a fair price while providing your organization with a return of at least 65% of the item's retail value.

The Silent Auction can generate 20% or more of your net profits.

Accompanying each item is a bid sheet and pen. The bid sheet provides information about the item, donor, and minimum bid increment, and has lined spaces for guests to write their Bid Card numbers beside their bid amounts (see page 186).

A Silent Auction is a timed event. Bidding is closed at a specified time. Guests can place as many bids on an item as they wish up until the closing time.

Assuming there are many items in the Silent Auction, they are often divided into two or three sections with each section closing at a different time. Sections are usually identified by color—the Red Section may close at 9 pm, the Green Section at 9:15 pm, and the Blue Section at 9:30 pm.

To help 'compress' the bidding activity, items of the same color should be grouped in the same area of the room. This makes it easy for guests who are bidding on several items in the same section.

Guests place a bid by increasing the amount of the previous bid on the sheet and writing down the amount of their bid on the next line of the bid sheet. Minimum bid increments of at least $5-10 (or more on larger items) are strongly recommended.

Bidders are identified by their Bid Card number (a Bid Card number should be issued to each guest at registration).

The person who places the last and highest bid on the bid sheet wins the item, as long as the final bid meets the minimum bid increment requirement.

TALKING POINT

● Silent Auction bid sheets should never request or require phone numbers due to privacy and security issues.

FEATURES AND BENEFITS OF SILENT AUCTIONS

▶ Numerous items can be merchandized at the same time

▶ Silent Auctions are easy to organize

▶ Everyone can participate—generally there is an interesting variety of items with a wide range of monetary values

▶ Silent Auctions are normally low-pressure events suitable for all guests

▶ Silent Auctions are entertaining and engaging, and they can extract considerable revenue; typically they generate 65% or more of an item's retail value and can provide 20% or more of your net profits

Because a higher percentage of your guests will participate in the Silent Auction than the Live Auction, let's take a more in-depth look at organizing a profitable Silent Auction.

ORGANIZING A SUCCESSFUL SILENT AUCTION

The Silent Auction chair will need lots of help—you will want to assemble a committee of energetic, fun-loving volunteers. Each volunteer will have a specific and important role to play.

Organization Chart for Silent Auctions

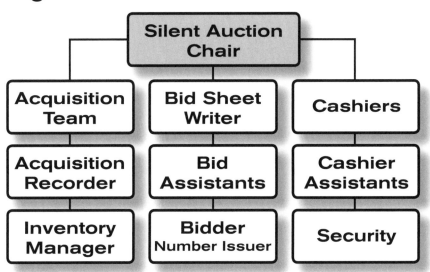

Silent Auction Chair

This individual is in charge of assembling, training, and managing an energetic group of volunteers to fill the key positions outlined in the Silent Auction organization chart. The Silent Auction chair represents this group at all meetings of the event steering committee. The chair must be able to oversee the entire Silent Auction and answer all questions that arise.

Acquisition Team

These volunteers will participate in an acquisition brainstorming session with the Live Auction acquisition team members, the idea being to create a list of potential items and donors for both auctions.

The volunteers will have tools available to make the job easier, including my list of 400 Great Auction Items (see Chapter Eight); a list of last year's donors; a list of prospective new donors; sample solicitation letters; telephone prospecting scripts; and so on.

How many acquisition team volunteers are required?

We recommend:

▶ two teams of two volunteers for up to 500 guests

▶ two teams of four volunteers for 500 to 1,000 guests

▶ three teams of four volunteers for more than 1,000 guests

Acquisition Recorder

This volunteer receives items from the acquisition team along with the Auction Acquisition Form (see page 182) that accompanies each donation. The acquisition recorder enters each item into an auction donation spreadsheet, which can be either computerized or manual, depending on size of event and preference.

A number is assigned to each item and a numbered label or dot attached to each item as it comes in. This number is recorded on the auction acquisition form.

To ensure maximum control over items being received, only one person should fill this position. This person should write thank-you letters to the donors of items, and issue tax receipts if applicable.

Inventory Manager

When the items have been recorded, they are turned over to the inventory manager for safekeeping. This person should:

▶ Place the item in safekeeping until the event

▶ Place Silent Auction Acquisition Forms in one of two folders or binders; one marked Item Received if you have the item, one marked Item Pending for items committed but not yet received

► Follow up on items pending by calling donors with a friendly reminder

► Arrange for pick up or delivery of items pending

► Ensure that all items are delivered to the event site and accounted for on event day

► After the event, secure all items left behind by purchasers or not sold

TALKING POINT

❛ **Items not sold at the event can be used for volunteer gifts, or stored away for next year.**

Bid Sheet Writer

A bid sheet needs to be prepared for each item in the Silent Auction. These are easily prepared using auction software, a spreadsheet program like Excel, or a word processing program like Microsoft Word (using tables).

Only one individual is required for the bid sheet writer position, but this volunteer needs an eye for detail to ensure that bid sheets are filled out accurately. Each bid sheet will be numbered to coordinate with the numbered label or dot on each auction item.

As well, the bid sheet writer may have to create attractive gift certificates to display for donated services. For example, a trucker who has offered a load of gravel probably won't provide an actual gift certificate or anything that would be suitable for display.

Bid sheets are usually color-coded (using a colored dot or colored paper) to identify their closing time in the Silent Auction. Each sheet also typically includes:

► Item description—keep this brief and to the point

► Special conditions (such as Blackout Dates)

▶ Item value (optional - see my discussion about this on page 51)

▶ Minimum bid increment ($5-10 on smaller items, higher for larger items)

▶ Minimum opening bid (optional, and never higher than 50% of the item's value)

▶ Lined spaces for bid number, bid amount, and perhaps the bidder's initials or signature

TALKING POINT

Three-copy carbonless paper works great for bid sheets—at closing time one copy goes to the cashier, one copy to the buyer, and one copy stays with the item until pickup.

Bid Assistants

The primary duty of the bid assistants is to watch over the items and ensure their security. In addition, the bid assistants must make certain that:

▶ There is a bid sheet for each item on the table

▶ A pen is placed by each bid sheet—remove the lid so people don't take the pen

▶ Bid sheets remain in place until the Silent Auction closes

▶ No merchandise is removed without being paid for

Bid assistants must also make sure there are no spaces for bids left on the bottom of the bid sheet before it is flipped over (if using a two-sided format). If any spaces have been skipped, the bid assistant should strike a line through that space.

When both the front and/or back of the bid sheet is 90% full the bid assistant should replace it, ensuring that the information on the new sheet is accurate and that it is set up correctly. The highest bid on the old sheet must be entered as the first bid on the new sheet.

When the Silent Auction closes, the bid assistant either removes the bid sheet for each item or otherwise identifies the successful bidder. If necessary, the bid assistant must complete the bid sheet by filling in the successful bidder's number and bid amount at the top of the bid sheet.

Depending on the style of bid sheet being used, the bid assistant gives either the bid stub or a copy of the three-carbon bid sheet to an event coordinator assistant or runner to be immediately taken to the cashier for processing.

When the guests are ready to pick up their items, the bid assistant must make sure that each guest has a receipt for the item being collected. They must also make sure the guest signs the top portion of the bid sheet to acknowledge that the goods have been received. The signed bid sheet is then sent to the cashier for filing.

If delivery of items is available, the bid assistant will collect delivery details and write them on the bid sheet.

There should be one bid assistant assigned to each table of Silent Auction items. If that isn't possible, my rule of thumb is to have at least two bid assistants for every three Silent Auction tables set up along a wall, and at least four bid assistants for tables in a horseshoe setup.

Bidder Number Issuer

A bidder number should be assigned to each guest. Usually pre-printed on a Bid Card, the bidder number corresponds to the number on the bidder registration form, which also includes the guest's name, contact information, payment preference, and possibly encrypted credit card information if using an express payment system.

Bidder numbers can be issued automatically to each guest at the time of registration and included in guest registration packages. Alternatively, a separate station can be set up to issue bidder numbers if this is not handled at the registration desk.

You should decide ahead of time if all guests will be issued bidder numbers (which I think is a smart idea), or if a bidder number will be issued only at the request of guests wishing to participate in the Live or Silent auctions.

Guests can also fill out self-registered Bid Cards. These Bid Cards have a perforated line separating two parts. One part has space where guests can fill out their personal information, and the other part has the bidder number printed on it. Guests can fill out their personal information, then tear that part off and hand it to the bidder number issuer. The part with the bidder number is kept and used during the auctions. These self-registering Bid Cards are a great time-saver.

TALKING POINT

● **The number of volunteers required for the bidder number issuer position will depend on the number of attendees and the type of Bid Card being used.**

Cashiers

The cashier's role is simple, but not necessarily easy. These individuals are dealing with all of the cash, check, credit, and debit receipts. Accuracy and attention to detail are absolutely essential. Experience is preferable—it makes sense to select individuals with banking, accounting, bookkeeping, or retail backgrounds to fill the cashier positions.

There can be a lot of pressure at the end of an event. Guests want to pay for their purchases and leave. It is critical that an efficient system is in place, and that all cashiers are absolutely familiar with how the system works. Each cashier should have his or her own station equipped with:

▶ Cashbox and float

▶ Credit and debit card scanner, or credit card imprint machine

► Calculator

► Stapler with extra staples (for attaching credit card slips or cash to item sheets)

► Highlighter pens

► Pens, paperclips, and other supplies

Cashier Assistants

You should have a team of three volunteers working to assist the cashiers. Their duties are as follows:

One volunteer manages the auction donation spreadsheet. As items are closed, their sale prices are recorded on the spreadsheet.

The second volunteer sorts the bid sheets or cards by the successful bidder number.

The third volunteer writes up a receipt for each winning bidder. When the bidder comes to a cashier to pay for the purchase, the volunteer hands the cashier everything needed to complete the transaction.

TALKING POINT

Fundraising auction software makes this task much easier.

Security

Depending on the size and nature of your event, it may be a good idea to hire professional security personnel, or have specific volunteers assume these roles, to keep an eye on the auction displays, particularly where valuable items like jewelry are exposed.

HOW TO CLOSE THE SILENT AUCTION

Guests must be properly advised of the Silent Auction closing times. This can be done in several ways.

▶ Closing times can be printed in the catalog

▶ Closing times can be posted on signage and displayed around the room

▶ Closing times can be displayed on video screens

▶ If using video screens, a computerized countdown clock can be used

▶ Closing times can be announced by the emcee

▶ Closing times can be printed right on the bid sheets

Good methods for closing the bidding include using a highlighter to strike through the last and highest bid on the bid sheet (after ensuring it meets the minimum bid increment). You can also circle the winning bid and tear off the top copy of the bid sheet if carbonless forms are being used, or you can simply remove the bid sheet from the table and take it to the cashier station for inputting.

Another idea is to affix a pre-printed adhesive label on the bid sheet that reads, "This Item Is Now Closed—Please Proceed to Cashier."

How do bidders know if they've been successful?

▶ Names of winners can be posted on a video screen or on a white board

▶ Bidders can look to see if their name or bid number are highlighted as the winning bid on the bid sheet

▶ Winner's names can be announced (although this is absolutely the least effective method and should be discussed in advance with your emcee and/or auctioneer)

▲ With David Foster at the 25th Anniversary Gala of the David Foster Foundation in Victoria, BC, where his piano (autographed by 120 sport and entertainment luminaries) was auctioned for $500,000

▲ An example of excellent signage that conveys important information to guests upon their arrival

▲ A great sign, but a half-hour between closings is usually far too long

◀ Investigate preregistration of credit cards as an effective means of speeding up the check-out process at the end of the event

▼ Another simple but effective way to inform guests of Silent Auction closing times

Auctions/Raffles General Terms

1. Payment for all items must be made tonight by cash, personal cheque or credit card.
2. Final lists of auction and raffle items may change between program printing and this evening's event.
3. All items sold "as is".

Live Auction Guidelines

1. Successful bidders must sign an "Acknowledgement of Purchase" as soon as the article is sold.
2. If a bid is disputed, the bid will re-open at the discretion of the Auctioneer whose decision is final.

Silent Auction Rules

1. All items have bid sheets affixed nearby. To "bid" on an item, legibly print your name and bid price with your signature and phone number on the respective sheet.
2. Each bid must increase by the amount indicated as the minimum increment on the bid sheet.
3. The closing bid will be certified by a Hospice Gala Committee Member.
4. The last signature on a bid sheet will constitute the winning bid and is binding upon the bidder.

▲ If you're planning a Super Silent Auction, special signage like this is absolutely essential

▲ Any sign shop can easily produce beautiful displays like this one, which really help promote your auction items

◀ Auction rules are typically printed in the auction catalog or event program. As an option, a large sign can be displayed in the reception area

87

◀ This is better. Volunteers have done a wonderful job decorating this Wine Tree and tying it to the event theme

▲ A "bare-bones" Wine Tree display. Thank goodness for the sign!

▼ This is an interesting photo. Notice that the signage acknowledges the wine donors

▶ This is a seven-tier Wine Tree being used in a Silent Auction with guests able to place bids on individual tiers. "The higher the tier, the better the wine" often works well in this case

WINE TREE PLANS

Constructed of plywood, this Wine Tree is designed to hold 100 bottles of wine & spirits. It can be draped in fabric, lights, etc.

Top tier - 8" round sits over 3.5" x 3.5" base piece

Riser #1 - 5" x 5" x 13"H

Tier #2 - 16" round

Riser #2 - 10" x 10" x 13"H

Tier #3 - 24" round

Riser #3 - 14" x 14" x 13"H

Tier #4 - 32" round

Riser #4 - 20" x 20" x 13"H

Tier #5 - 40" round

Base - 23.5" x 23.5" x 26"H

◀ View beneath each tier

▼ Base pieces hold each riser in place

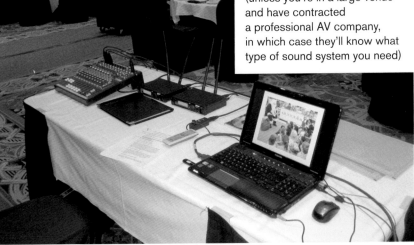

▲ This is a large AV set-up with professional technicians at a major gala-style event. Regardless the size of your event, it's ALWAYS a good idea to have an audio technician present

◀ This is an example of a powered PA speaker raised on a stand, and is a CRITICAL component of a successful fundraising auction. Don't let anybody tell you otherwise (unless you're in a large venue and have contracted a professional AV company, in which case they'll know what type of sound system you need)

▲ This set-up illustrates the bare minimum for proper AV equipment—a small audio mixer, receiver(s) for cordless microphone(s), and a computer for the PowerPoint display. Don't forget to make arrangements for background and dinner music. An iPod or similar device (with appropriate playlists) plugged into the audio mixer gives you total control of the background music, which is important

▲ A perfect podium! Plenty of room for notes, a lip to keep them from sliding off, and a shelf for holding extra notes, props, batteries, water, awards, etc.

▲ Note the placement of the microphones on this podium. They prevent the emcee or auctioneer from opening a binder and laying it flat. Also, the pitch is too steep for using a computer on this surface. On the plus side, the small table is perfect for holding water, towel, microphone, or a computer

▲ An excellent example of stage lighting and decoration at a major gala

▼ Same event, different year. Incredible staging!

▲ This picture illustrates the importance of proper lighting on the stage area

◀ An example of a Mid Tier Cash Appeal. Guests make a pledge in exchange for a puzzle piece which they then place on the board

▲ The fully-assembled puzzle, evidence of another very successful Cash Appeal

▲ A congested Silent Auction display that makes it very difficult for guests to figure out what is being offered and what they're actually bidding on

▼ Yikes, more congestion! Ideally, try to allow two lineal feet of space between Silent Auction bid sheets

▲ A picture says a thousand words. It would be difficult to improve on this Silent Auction display

◄ Now THIS is a perfect Silent Auction display! Plenty of space and the auction item is tagged with an ID number that corresponds to a number on the bid sheet and tent card. Attractive, attention-grabbing, and no confusion

▲ A very creative icebreaker auction item – the opportunity to upgrade to this First-Class VIP table

▲ In addition to waiter service, premium wines, and an upgraded dinner menu, the purchaser of this VIP table went home with all these gorgeous table settings and decorations

▲ Strategically placed close to the stage, these are definitely the "best seats in the house." In the background, Live Auction items are displayed with both signage and PowerPoint

▲ A hard-working volunteer counts the cash collected prior to a Purse Snatcher auction...then prepares to hide it in one of the purses that will be auctioned

▶ Entertain, Engage, and Extract...that's the objective when trying something new

◀ The Purse Snatcher auction is a proven winner and always a crowd-pleaser

▲ Here's a setup for a Diamond Mine raffle. Again, an idea that fulfills the 3 E's of a successful fundraiser—Entertain, Engage, Extract

▶ Guests hope to scoop the winning bead, but in case nobody does, be sure to provide each participant a numbered draw ticket

▲ The $100 Signature technique—another form of Mid Tier Cash Appeal that often works very well with an original painting

▲ A very clever way to merchandize the Live Auction items; informative, get-to-the-point signage accompanied by PowerPoint displays

◄ A little merchandizing goes a long way. Use your imagination and get creative. Think of those great window displays at the shopping mall and how they grab your attention

◄ Here's that bottle of fine wine autographed by the entire Calgary Flames hockey team, smartly displayed under a glass case that elevated this auction item to "gallery" status. The end result…$17,000!

▲ The amazing craftsmanship of woodcarver Clay Simpson. This and other lifelike (and life-size) animal carvings were featured auction items for many years at the Calgary Zoo Tusks & Tails Gala, and generated hundreds of thousands of dollars

◀ Can you believe this is actually a cake? It turned into a Hot Potato auction item and raised thousands of dollars in a single evening

▲ I've seen many interesting Silent Auction items over the years, but this was a strange one...a box of explosives!

▼ An absolute First-Class raffle for an awesome prize. This couple roamed through the room and quickly sold all the raffle tickets. Note the excellent signage and the POS machine that enabled the effortless collection of credit card payments. Even the raffle tickets on the tray...well done!

▲ Another creative raffle presentation... goody bags combined with a balloon pop. Again, use your imagination and don't be afraid to get creative

◄ Miss Rodeo Canada holds a framed photo that raised almost $20,000 in a Mid Tier Cash Appeal using the $1,000 signature technique

◀ As a Live or Silent auction item, or even as a raffle prize, lotto trees are always popular. Be sure to confirm the legality of raffles and draws in your jurisdiction

▼ These school kids created hand-painted lunch boxes that raised a whopping $30,000 in ten minutes during a Cash Appeal at a Rotary Club auction

▲ This was a crazy day. I sold Don Cherry's framed jacket for $5,000 at a hockey fundraiser, then the shirt off my back (literally) for $7,500!

▲ The #1 complaint at fundraising auction events is "long checkout lineups at the end of the evening." This common problem can be avoided, in part by having plenty of properly-trained cashiers ready to go

▶ An example of a well-equipped cashier station. For info on Checkout Procedures visit **www.symphonycb.com**

▲ This is just a very cool picture of the friendly staff and fantastic decorations at a Festival of Trees event

◄ Ladies love shoes. This exhausted volunteer brought two pairs to this event!

▼ All smiles following another successful fundraising auction in support of Canadian medical missions to Ecuador

▲ This has to be one of the all-time coolest names (and themes) for a fundraising auction event, courtesy of Rotarian Jeff Polovick

◀ A hard-working volunteer self-medicating at the end of a successful fundraising auction event

SILENT AUCTION
SUCCESS STRATEGIES

The importance of setting goals for your Silent Auction cannot be overstated. Early in the process, the Silent Auction committee should establish these goals. Having a bulls eye to aim at helps keep everyone focused and motivated.

You will need to establish goals for:

▶ The amount of money you wish to raise in the Silent Auction

▶ The number of items and retail dollar value of items you need to collect for your Silent Auction, knowing that you can expect to receive at least 65% of retail value from a well-planned Silent Auction

Goals can be established in two ways—based on a specific need, or based on a budget.

Let's say your organization is raising money for a specific need. For example, it is going to cost $25,000 to send a school class on a field trip to France. A specific dollar amount is needed, and thus your goal becomes that specific amount of money.

Now let's say your fundraising efforts are ongoing and open-ended. For example, your organization supports several worthwhile initiatives in the community each year. Think of a church group raising funds for missions in Africa, or a Rotary Club raising money for a hot-lunch program. There is no end and no limit to the amount of resources that are needed.

Building a budget naturally leads to a profit number, and this number becomes your event goal. For example, you may decide that the Silent Auction will contribute $5,000 toward this event goal. Knowing that a Silent Auction typically generates 65% of retail value, you will need to solicit roughly $7,800 (retail value) worth of auction items.

How many items should be in your Silent Auction?

The rule of thumb is to have one to 1.5 items for every couple attending the auction.

Let's say there are 200 guests attending your event, equal to one hundred couples. If there are one hundred items in your Silent Auction, these items should have an average retail value of $78 to produce the $5,000 needed for the Silent Auction's contribution to event goal.

Put another way: 100 items @ $78 = $7,800 X .65 = $5,070

Of course these numbers are approximate, but they illustrate that it's a good idea to think about and plan your auction acquisitions.

Consider this—there is limited buying power in the room and people have only so much money to spend, although we never know what that number is. Spreading this limited buying power over too many items creates a **buyer's market** and diminishes the Return On Investment (ROI) of your Silent Auction. This means your entire team has worked harder at acquiring donations, but for much less money.

Conversely, too few items in your Silent Auction creates a **seller's market**. It does not allow sufficient opportunities for guests to spend as much as they might have were there more items to choose from.

The point is that it is better to concentrate on soliciting high-quality, interesting items for your Silent Auction than it is to focus on mediocre items. Imagine that you're opening a new store that is only going to be open for four hours. What kind of stock do you want to put on the shelves? What kind of store are you— a Wal-Mart or Macy's?

Many times Silent Auction tables are filled with cheap items that nobody is all that interested in buying, and if they do buy these items they certainly won't pay much money for them.

This defeats the purpose of the Silent Auction, which is to provide guests with the opportunity to purchase a few great items at a fair price while providing your organization with a return of 65% or higher.

If you have a variety of related items (golf shirt, golf balls, putter, ball cap, gift certificate from a pro shop, green fees to a golf course), you can bundle these items together as a themed package. This will reduce the number of boring small items in your Silent Auction and help generate higher returns—a classic example of the sum being greater than the total of its parts.

Make your displays as creative and attractive as possible, using desktop publishing software to design eye-catching tent cards and gift certificates.

Every Silent Auction display has four components—the item being sold (this may be a photo and description on a poster board) including a clearly displayed item number on a label or adhesive dot, which of course corresponds to the same number on the bid sheet; a tent card with a brief description (use large print and bullets) of the item along with the item number; the bid sheet with the item number; and a pen (removing the lid reduces the likelihood of the pen being taken).

Part of the fun of a Silent Auction is walking around and looking over all the offerings. Everybody likes to window shop. Some of the things that can add sizzle to a Silent Auction display include:

► Good lighting

► Baskets, cellophane, ribbons, and bows

► Poster board displays

► Effective use of color

► Placing items on draped boxes to create "skylines"

► Effective signage and attractive gift certificates

SETTING UP

Whenever possible, the Silent Auction should be set up in the same room as the Live Auction, on tables set around perimeter walls. Depending on the available space, tables may be set in a variety of configurations—horseshoe, rectangular pods, T-shape, H-shape, and so on. These tables should not interfere with the auctioneer's sight lines during the Live Auction.

Make sure there are enough tables to display all of the items without crowding either the items or the guests who are bidding on the items. Two feet of lineal table space per item is recommended.

FINDING ITEMS TO SELL IN YOUR SILENT AUCTION

Silent Auction items typically come from three sources:

▶ Donations

▶ Consignments

▶ Purchased items
  - Using donor cash
  - Using a budgeted cash advance

Where do you start? The following ideas may help.

Hold a brainstorming session—Think outside the box. Invite up to a dozen people (committee members, friends, whoever) and have some fun. Eat pizza, drink wine, and get creative. Let your imaginations run wild as you ask, "What are some really cool ideas for Silent Auction items?"

Have someone chair this session. Ideas can be collected and recorded on flip charts with sheets torn off as they're filled, then hung around the room for all to see. Connect the dots—and remember, there are no bad ideas.

Use the 400 Great Auction Items list in Chapter Eight to prompt your imagination and get your creative juices flowing.

Auction items fall into three basic categories:

▶ Goods and consumables (home electronics, fine wine)

▶ Services (laser eye surgery, estate planning)

▶ Experiences (exotic travel, cooking lessons)

The number-one rule when soliciting auction items is this: Don't be afraid to ask!

Ask the question, "Who knows who?"—As you create a list of exciting auction items, go down the list and examine each item, then ask the group, "Who knows somebody who could possibly donate this item, or who could help us get to somebody who can make this donation?"

For example, let's say you are looking for Super Bowl tickets. Maybe your high school football coach knows a college coach who knows an NFL coach who knows somebody connected to the Super Bowl. Again, don't be afraid to ask!

Develop an action plan to connect with donors—there are two basic types of potential donors, network contacts and cold contacts, and you need a plan to connect with them.

Network contacts are warm prospects. A network contact may be someone you know personally, or someone known by someone you know. Regardless, conversations with warm prospects are always easier to initiate.

Cold contacts may be individuals or businesses you do not know. To find these contacts you can use phone books, business directories, and email or mailing lists. You can attend networking events, offer to speak at service club luncheons, or explore the potential of social media.

When soliciting cold contacts, it is absolutely critical to have your pitch well prepared. It needs to be brief and to the point, and most importantly, you need to make your request specific.

> ## TALKING POINT
>
> ● Many businesses budget money each year for charitable giving. This money is available to qualifying non-profits, so don't be afraid to ask for it.

SUPER SILENT AUCTIONS

A real money-maker, one of the best ideas ever, is called the Super Silent Auction.

Super Silent Auctions provide a way to merchandize premium items in the Silent Auction format. By premium items, I mean items that could have been included in the Live Auction but weren't because of time constraints (remember, eight to twelve items is typically enough for a fabulous Live Auction).

Super Silent Auction items must be set up on a separate table in a prominent area of the room, and the table must be well-lit. A large Super Silent Auction sign (at least three feet by four feet) hanging above the display table makes it easy for the emcee and auctioneer to direct attention to these special premium items.

Limit the number of items in the Super Silent Auction to no more than twenty. These items—and their donors—get extra attention in the catalog, on the special signage, and from the emcee and auctioneer throughout the event.

Walk-away Bid Sheets

Walk-away bid sheets are wonderful tools to help increase the revenue from your Super Silent Auction. These sheets are recommended for high-demand, subjective-value items like fine wines or romantic getaways. Guests pay a premium price for these items, but they don't mind—they get the item they want.

If a guest really wants to purchase an item, he or she may do so by placing their bidder number in a special walk-away bid box on the bid sheet. The guest instantly wins the bidding war.

The walk-away bid sheet saves the guest the effort of having to monitor competing bids on the item. People will often pay for the luxury of being able to buy exactly what they want without having to jump up and down all night, or having to worry about being outbid by someone else. They are also an excellent way to include and serve guests who must leave the event early.

Green **A-162**	**ITEM:** Romantic Weekend at Jasper Park Lodge	**VALUE:** **$ 1,000**

Special Conditions: Blah, blah, blah...

Bidder Number

	$200
	$300
	$400
	$500
	$600
	$700
	$800
	$900

Bidder Number

	$1,000
	$1,100
	$1,200
	$1,300
	$1,400

Bidder Number **Walk-away Bid**

	$1,500

How it works:

There are fourteen bid boxes on the bid sheet. Each bid box has a blank space for a bidder number to be entered, with a dollar value attached to each box. For example, the first bid box can begin at 20% of the item's value, with each subsequent box increasing the item's value by 10%. The final box (number fourteen) is valued at 150% of the item's value.

These percentage increases are discretionary and can be determined by the organizing committee, but don't get crazy.

The actual value of the item may or may not be stated on the bid sheet. It's optional.

The walk-away bid sheet is removed from the table as soon as somebody meets the walk-away bid price. At that point, the item is sold.

> **TALKING POINT**
>
> I've seen Walk-away Bid Sheets work with great success at countless auctions. Try it with a few items at your next event, even in the regular Silent Auction. There's nothing to lose.

CHAPTER 4
RAFFLES

Raffles are an excellent tool for generating additional profits at your event, and they fulfill each of the three E's—**Entertain, Engage, Extract.**

TALKING POINT

Be sure to check with your local gaming authority to see if you need a raffle license or permit. Raffles, draws, and other games of chance are regulated in many jurisdictions, and illegal in some.

Here are some of the most popular, and productive, raffles that I've seen.

HEADS OR TAILS RAFFLE

This raffle works best as an icebreaker played early in the evening. It is fast to execute and fun to watch. Guests buy in for the chance to win a nice prize by playing an engaging game of Heads or Tails.

What is the right time to do a raffle?

Do the raffle draws after the Silent Auctions have closed. This brings guests back to their seats and allows the volunteers and cashiers much-needed time to process all the Silent Auction bid sheets and prepare to process payments. Following this suggestion helps reduce congestion at the cash-out table at the end of the evening.

How it works:

You don't even need tickets for this. During the cocktail reception volunteers mingle with the guests and sell them a chance to play the Heads or Tails Raffle, normally for $10 to $20. If the guest buys in, the volunteer places a sticky dot on the person. The dot identifies the guest as qualified to play, and it prevents the guest from being pestered by other ticket sellers.

At some time during the event (shortly after they've been seated is often a good time), the guests who bought into the Heads or Tails Raffle are asked to stand. They are then instructed by the emcee to make a choice—heads or tails—and they indicate their choice by placing their hands on their heads or on their butts.

A volunteer is brought forward to toss a coin, and the outcome is announced. If it is heads, those people with their hands on their heads remain standing, while the tails sit down.

Those still standing are then asked to choose again—heads or tails? The process is repeated until only a few guests are left standing, at which time the remaining guests are invited onto the stage for the final few coin tosses.

It doesn't take long to get to the winner. The prize can be 50% of the Heads or Tails Raffle sales, or some other nice prize.

50/50 RAFFLE

A two-piece ticket or double-strip ticket is sold to guests for a fixed price. Individual tickets usually sell anywhere from $2 to $20, but may go as high as $50 to $100 at a major gala event. Discounts are usually offered as an incentive to purchase multiple tickets—one ticket for $5 or five tickets for $20, for example.

The purchaser retains one half of the two-piece ticket or half of the strip ticket; the ticket seller retains the other half and deposits these into a draw barrel.

At the end of the sale period one ticket is drawn from the draw barrel and the winning number is announced. The winner receives 50% of all the monies collected in the sale of the 50/50 tickets.

BUCKET RAFFLE

Prizes are lined up and displayed on a table. A container, usually a plastic pail or cardboard box, is placed in front of each prize.

Strips of ten tickets (may be more or less) are sold to guests at whatever price the organizers decide. Buyers then deposit their tickets in the container that accompanies the prize they hope to win. The buyer may deposit all their tickets into one container, a single ticket into ten different containers, or a few tickets each into several containers.

At a predetermined time a single winning ticket is drawn from each of the containers, and the winning ticket number is announced.

TALKING POINT

This raffle is a lot of fun because it gives the guests their choice of the prizes they would like to win, plus the opportunity to increase their chances of winning those prizes. As well, they have a chance to win more than one prize if their tickets are drawn from more than one container.

BALLOON-POP RAFFLE

Helium-filled balloons are sold to guests. Inside each balloon is a small piece of paper. After all the balloons have been sold, and following a countdown from the emcee, guests pop their balloons and retrieve the pieces of paper.

On one piece of paper are the words, "Congratulations, you've won the grand prize!"

The other pieces of paper may announce smaller prizes, or simply say, "Thanks for your support."

At one of the events I do each year, one hundred balloons are sold. A local jeweler donates a lovely diamond necklace as the grand prize, and $100 gift certificates to his store for each of the other ninety-nine balloons. I would imagine that only a small percentage of the gift certificates are redeemed. Nonetheless, it's a great promotion for this generous business owner. The hundred balloons always sell out at $100 each, netting a windfall of $10,000 for this non-profit organization.

This can be an entertaining, engaging addition to your event... and one with a high extraction rate.

TALKING POINTS

● Remember to pop the balloons before the Live Auction, so they are not blocking the sight lines of the auctioneer.

● How many balloons should you blow up and sell? Depends on the number of guests attending your event. Remembering the principle of supply and demand— if there are fewer balloons available and the prize is a good one, you can charge a higher price per balloon. Having said that, never have more than one balloon per couple available. The last thing you want is unsold balloons with one of them possibly containing the grand prize.

● If somebody's balloon soars to the ceiling, then what? If all balloons have been sold but the prize is unclaimed, you can assume the balloon that sailed away is the winner. If there are several balloons high in the rafters, have the owners of those balloons come onstage to participate in a draw for the winner.

For this reason alone, it's a great idea to provide a numbered ticket to each guest that purchases a balloon, with corresponding numbered tickets placed in a draw barrel should a draw become necessary.

BIG-BOY TOY RAFFLE

A limited number of tickets (say, for example, fifty tickets) are sold at a premium price (e.g. $200 each) for the chance to win one of three big-boy toys on display at the event—perhaps a new snowmobile, dirt bike, and quad.

How it works:

Ask the dealer supplying the toys for a pure donation of the machine that is won. If the dealer says no, ask for a "half-of-wholesale" purchase price on the machine along with the right to find a co-sponsor who will pay the other half of the wholesale price. This way, the dealer recovers 50% of the cost of the machine while still reaping huge publicity.

Now go find one or more co-sponsors for this high-profile, attention-grabbing raffle.

If you can't find a co-sponsor, your organization may agree to pay the other half-of-wholesale cost to the dealer out of ticket proceeds. Either way, your organization wins big.

Suppose the winner chooses the quad, and that a half-of-wholesale price of $3,000 was pre-negotiated with the dealer. Ticket sales generated $10,000, realizing a profit of $7,000 for the charity.

But what if a third party has co-sponsored this raffle by agreeing to cover the $3,000 dealer cost? Now the windfall to the charity is the full $10,000!

TALKING POINTS

This raffle works like magic with the right crowd, appealing to the gambling instincts of guests (usually guys) who perceive that a one-in-fifty chance to win a $10,000 toy is well worth the $200 investment.

● Add another layer of excitement (and revenue) to this raffle by offering an Option Auction (see page 129) to three semi-finalists drawn from the draw barrel and now standing onstage. The audience loves this.

● Audience excitement and participation is high, especially when the moment comes for the winner to choose his (or her) toy. This is another winning raffle idea— Entertaining, Engaging, and high Extraction...the three E's!

GOLDEN TICKET RAFFLE

This is also called a First Choice Raffle. Guests purchase a numbered ticket for a chance to win first choice of any one item from either the Live or Silent auctions. Obviously, this draw takes place prior to the start of the Live Auction. As with all raffles, the price of the tickets should reflect the value of the prizes.

TALKING POINT

● You may choose to withhold a particular item from this raffle. However, the exclusion from this raffle of any item in the Live or Silent auctions must be well advertised at the time tickets are being sold.

CENTERPIECE RAFFLE

Flowers and other attractive or interesting centerpieces make excellent prizes for table raffles.

How it works:

An envelope containing a pencil and slips of paper, one per guest, is placed at each table.

Guests are invited to place a cash donation in the envelope and write their name on a slip of paper. The cash donations and slips of paper are returned to the envelope. One person at the table draws a name from the envelope, and that person gets to take the centerpiece home.

GREAT IDEA!

There is an even better way to collect the names of guests wishing to participate in the centerpiece raffle. I like this method because it saves people the hassle of messing around with slips of paper. With this method, the only thing inside the envelopes is the cash.

Print the following text on the front of each self-adhesive envelope:

Centerpiece Raffle

"Please place your donation inside the envelope, then pick a number and print your name on the corresponding line. Later in the evening, the winning number will be announced. Thank you for your generous donation."

1. _____
2. _____
3. _____
4. _____
5. _____
6. _____
7. _____
8. _____
9. _____
10. _____

After depositing a donation in the envelope, guests simply write their name on a line and wait for the emcee to draw the winning number (one through ten) from a fishbowl. If the lucky number is eight, for example, every person in the room who wrote their name on line number eight is a winner.

Volunteers then collect the cash envelopes from each table.

TALKING POINTS

● If the floral centerpieces were delivered in boxes, store those boxes under the table until the winner is ready to leave the event, at which point they can retrieve the box for their centerpiece.

● The emcee should mention that participation in this raffle is optional. Some people feel pressured and uncomfortable when asked to participate in a centerpiece raffle. They may not be carrying cash; they may feel like they're being "nickel and dimed;" or they may simply not like the centerpiece. It is never a good thing when guests feel awkward, pressured, or embarrassed.

TREASURE CHEST RAFFLE

Guests purchase a key to a locked treasure chest that contains mystery prizes. If the key unlocks the chest, they win the prizes.

TALKING POINTS

● All but one of the keys are blanks that can be purchased in bulk at most hardware supply stores. There is only one key that opens the lock.

● Jewelry, gift certificates, and lotto tickets make great prizes for a treasure chest.

CHAMPAGNE & DIAMOND RAFFLE

Jewelers often like to sponsor this raffle. In this event, guests purchase a glass of champagne. Attached to each glass is a small pouch. Inside one of the pouches is a real diamond; all others contain a cubic zirconia.

At a predetermined time (when all the glasses have been sold, or at the end of the evening) guests return to the point of purchase where a gemologist is waiting to examine their stone. One lucky winner has the diamond. Guests get to keep the champagne glasses.

Alternatively, you could number each of the champagne glasses and hold a draw to pick the lucky number. In this format, the actual diamond remains on display at the point of purchase, eliminating the risk that it could be lost—or worse, as the following Associated Press news story, published on April 26, 2013, shows:

> *The idea behind the Tampa Women's Club charity event was simple. For $20, you could buy a flute of champagne and a chance to win a one-carat, $5,000 diamond.*
>
> *Organizers of the Saturday event placed $10 cubic zirconia stones in the bottom of 399 of the 400 champagne glasses. The prized diamond, donated by Continental Wholesale Diamonds, was placed in the last. The problem? Eighty-year-old Miriam Tucker accidentally swallowed it.*
>
> *Tucker told local news media that she didn't want to put her finger in the champagne, so she drank a bit. While laughing with women at the table, she realized she swallowed it.*
>
> *Embarrassed, she had to tell the jewelers who were frantically searching for the winner. Already scheduled for a colonoscopy on Monday, she had the doctor recover the jewel.*

TALKING POINT

● Consider having the champagne glasses engraved with your organization's logo.

LOTTO TREE RAFFLE

Guests buy a raffle ticket for the chance to win all of the lotto tickets hanging from an artificial tree on display in the main room of the event.

DIAMOND MINE RAFFLE

A portable sandbox is filled with sand, and a quantity of colored beads is mixed into the sand. Guests buy a numbered ticket that qualifies them to sift through the sand until they find a bead, which they keep.

The event organizer retains a duplicate of just one of the beads in the sandbox. Later in the evening, when a photo of the winning bead is displayed on a large screen, or is simply described by the emcee, the guests discover if their bead matches the duplicate bead.

The holder of the winning bead wins a prize, perhaps a piece of diamond jewelry.

TALKING POINTS

● If the winning bead is not scooped out of the sandbox and no one steps forward to claim the prize, a ticket draw can be held from the tickets that were sold.

● The emcee should have the duplicate bead onstage for verification purposes.

TEQUILA RAFFLE

Guests buy a ticket for a chance to win a trip to Mexico, or a night out at a Mexican restaurant, or perhaps a Margarita machine with a bottle of fine tequila. The point is that the prize should have a Mexican theme.

How it works:

Ten tickets are drawn from a fishbowl, and the holders of those ten tickets are called to the stage where there are ten shot glasses waiting. Nine of the shot glasses are filled with water and one is filled with tequila. After a countdown, each qualifier picks up their glass and takes a sip. The person with the tequila wins the prize.

TALKING POINT

Check with your local gaming authority on this one. At the very least, participants in this raffle must be of legal drinking age.

127

HYBRID RAFFLES

Hybrid raffles have an auction component attached to them. Here are a couple of my favorites:

STRIP FOR A TRIP

Ten strips of double-strip tickets are auctioned individually for the chance to win a trip. As soon as the first strip sells, the auctioneer offers the remaining strips at that price. Sometimes the successful bidder will purchase additional strips of tickets "times the money," meaning that whatever price was paid for the first strip will be paid for each additional strip.

If there are any strips left, the auction resumes. The process is re-peated until all ticket strips are sold. The auction portion works well for selling the tickets because people can buy their way into a one-in-ten chance of winning the prize.

One strip of each double-strip ticket sold is then deposited into a draw barrel, from which a single ticket is drawn. The person hold-ing the corresponding ticket wins the trip.

It really makes no difference whether a strip of tickets or a single ticket is auctioned off; the odds of winning don't change. Psycho-logically, however, most people believe they have a better chance of winning the prize if they have more tickets in the draw barrel.

People are funny.

TALKING POINT

● This raffle really works well when there is a great prize, such as a trip to New York or Las Vegas.

AUCTION OPTION RAFFLE

I came up with this nifty idea for generating extra revenue—sometimes thousands of extra dollars—for my clients.

How it works:

When drawing for a large raffle prize such as a cruise vacation, rather than draw just one winning ticket from the draw barrel, draw three tickets. These three people are now semi-finalists in the big draw.

However, before making the final draw, give each of the three semi-finalists the option to have their ticket auctioned off, with the proceeds divided as follows:

▶ After the ticket has been auctioned, the semi-finalist first recoups the full cost of his or her ticket

▶ The balance of the auction proceeds is then split fifty-fifty between the semi-finalist and the charity

Say a ticket was purchased for $100 and resold for $1,000. After the ticket holder recoups his or her investment of $100, the remaining $900 is split with the charity, an instant profit of $450. Not bad.

TALKING POINT

● From my personal experience, men are more likely to have their semi-finalist ticket auctioned off, with the chance of making an immediate gain. Women, on the other hand, are less likely to sell their ticket. They seem more content to stay in a draw with a one-in-three chance of winning. Nonetheless, this is an entertaining and engaging way to extract extra revenue.

CHAPTER 5
CASH APPEALS

Currently the hottest money-maker on the fundraising auction circuit, when properly executed, Cash Appeals (also called Fund-a-Need, Fund-a-Cause, Emotional Appeals, etc.) can work magic on your bottom line.

How It Works:

Simply ask for donations of money to support a particular initiative or specific need. The "ask" is made during your fundraising auction event, often in exchange for a charitable tax receipt if your organization is a registered non-profit.

Not all guests are interested in buying an item in the Live or Silent auctions. Regardless, people can often be motivated to open their wallets and make generous cash donations.

For Cash Appeals to work best, four things are required:

1. An emotional trigger—this can come from an impassioned speech or a well-produced short video that tugs at the heartstrings, creating that magic moment when guests wrap their heart around your cause

2. A well-presented pitch from the emcee, the auctioneer, a representative of the cause, or possibly even a committee member

3. A Bid Card number for each guest

4. Three clerks to record Bid Card numbers as they are called out by the emcee or auctioneer. The purpose of having three clerks is to prevent recording errors

There are three basic types of Cash Appeals—I refer to them as Top Tier, Mid Tier, and Bottom Tier appeals.

TOP-DOWN SWEEP (TOP TIER)

Following an emotional appeal during a speech or video, a special pitch is made by the emcee or auctioneer inviting guests to make pledges by raising their Bid Card numbers in the air, beginning with higher amounts of money and moving to lower amounts. These numbers are called out by the emcee or auctioneer and recorded by three different individuals, usually volunteers or auction clerks, to ensure accuracy (see page 185).

The recorded pledges are then taken to the cashier for processing.

TEAM SWEEP (MID TIER)

The auctioneer invites guests to make a specified pledge in exchange for an opportunity that makes them part of a select team. The opportunity may be to purchase one of a limited number of items, such as a piece of children's art or a puzzle piece. Or the opportunity may be to take an action, such as signing the back of a painting that will hang in the local hospital.

PERSONAL PLEDGE (BOTTOM TIER)

As an example of a personal pledge, you can place donation envelopes or pledge cards at each table setting, and ask guests to fill them out at their own discretion and in amounts of their choosing. However, this is typically the least effective method of Cash Appeal.

A more effective technique for collecting smaller pledges is similar to what you often see at grocery stores or banks, where customers are asked to make a donation and then write their names on a paper cut-out that hangs on the wall. I've seen this work with paper lobsters signed and taped to netting at a Rotary lobster-fest, and with Christmas stocking cut-outs signed and displayed on a Christmas tree at a Festival of Trees Gala.

Case Study #1
— Hand-Painted Lunch Boxes

Edmonton's Mayfield Rotary Club sponsors a hot-lunch program at Brightview School. Thirty of the elementary students, many from underprivileged, single-parent homes, were asked to hand-paint lunch boxes in their art class. The idea was that I would auction these hand-painted lunch boxes, hopefully for $100 each, at the annual Rotary auction.

On the evening of the event, the kids entered the hotel ballroom with their lunch boxes in hand and sang the national anthem. Then the school principal gave an impassioned speech, describing how most of these young children were arriving at school each morning with empty tummies and no lunches.

After the principal's speech there was barely a dry eye in the room. Just before starting the lunch box auction, I decided to ask if anyone would be generous enough to offer $1,000 for first choice of these unique art pieces.

To everyone's amazement, eight people immediately raised their hands.

"Come on up!" I said, encouraging others to follow. Before you knew it, twenty-six of the thirty lunch boxes had been snapped up... at $1,000 each!

At last, four disappointed little kids were left still holding their lunch boxes high. Cajoling the audience, I said, "What are the chances? The four *best* lunch boxes are still available!"

With that, the final four were quickly snapped up, turning what we had initially hoped would be a $3,000 auction attempt into a completely unplanned $30,000 Cash Appeal... in less than five minutes!

Case Study #2
— Art Smart

An artist had donated an original oil painting with a stated value of $2,500 to an auction supporting a local children's hospital. Unfortunately, nobody was interested in buying the abstract painting and bidding stalled at $200, an embarrassing situation given that the artist was in attendance.

Suddenly I had an idea. "This painting is much too valuable to sell for just $200," I said. "I'll be the first to throw in $100. Whoever joins me can sign the back of this painting, then we'll donate it to the children's hospital for all to enjoy."

To my surprise, forty-six people joined me by raising their hands and making a pledge, generating a total of $4,700 from a painting that was supposedly worth $2,500, but otherwise would have generated a measly $200.

Case Study #3
— A Compassionate Record

This was a big one. At a large gala event attended by many of the most successful business people in our community, money was being raised to pay down the mortgage on a new addition to Sorrentino's Compassion House, a 'home away from home' for out-of-town breast cancer patients visiting our city for treatment.

Falling $250,000 short of our goal, I made a bold plea to the audience, challenging them to see if twenty-five people would consider pledging $10,000 apiece in one minute or less. Not only would that set a new fundraising record, I announced, but we could end the evening mortgage-free.

To everyone's amazement, thirty-five people raised their hands. In roughly ninety seconds $350,000 was raised through this Cash Appeal, allowing full payment of the mortgage and then some.

The lesson? It never hurts to ask.

Case Study #4
— The High Cost of Gas

At an auction supporting our city's STARS air ambulance service, I interviewed a pilot onstage at the event and was surprised to learn that fuel for the helicopters costs $1,000 an hour. Thinking that this might be a perfect opportunity for an impromptu Cash Appeal, I asked how many people would consider pledging $1,000 to underwrite an hour's worth of fuel.

The first year I tried this idea it generated $17,000, the second year $25,000, and the third year $26,000.

The lesson? Watch for unexpected opportunities to launch a Cash Appeal.

Flop Sweat

My first experience doing a Cash Appeal (which turned out to be a real eye-opener and a great confidence builder) came during an event being held in Calgary, Alberta, in support of a local emergency shelter.

For whatever reason, the organizers did not send a list of auction items prior to the event, but I wasn't too worried; I can think on my feet. It wasn't until the executive director of the organization introduced me and I bounced up on stage that I began to worry.

"All right, Linda (not her real name), what's our first auction item?" I asked.

With a blank stare, she leaned over and whispered, "We don't have anything."

Sadly, this exchange (and my flop sweat) could be seen on the huge video screens flanking the stage.

"What would you like me to do?" I whispered back in a panicked tone.

"Just ask them for money!" she said. ... see over

So that's what I did. Turning to the audience, I said, "Folks, this is going to be a bit different than any other fundraising auction you've ever attended."

I was glad that Linda was still standing beside me onstage. Asking her to explain the mission of her organization gave me a minute or two to gather my thoughts and plan a strategy.

And then she mentioned an upcoming capital campaign to renovate the shelter. Sixteen guest rooms required renovations at a cost of $5,000 each.

Bingo!

Turning to the audience, I asked if anyone might consider underwriting the cost to renovate a single guestroom with the offer that a plaque would hang on the door saying, "This room was brightened by the Smith Family."

In no time at all we collected enough pledges to renovate all sixteen rooms, then continued on to collect money for a teen computer center, a kitchen renovation, etc.

By the time the dust settled twenty minutes later, almost $250,000 had been raised for the cause, all without a single auction item.

Go figure.

DASH FOR CASH

Need to make $5,000 (actually $5,050) in a hurry?
This technique is a veiled Cash Appeal called Dash for Cash.

Four flipcharts are placed on easels in each corner of the room, with each flipchart displaying two columns of twenty-five boxes, as illustrated. Numbers one through one hundred are written randomly in the left-hand columns of the four sheets, with twenty-five numbers on each sheet.

The best way to do this is to have four volunteers with markers stand at each flipchart prior to the event, each taking a sequential number as it is called out by a fifth volunteer and writing it in a left-hand square. The right-hand columns are left blank at this time.

At some point during the event, guests are invited to race to a flip-chart and write their Bid Card numbers in a box that corresponds to the dollar amount they would be prepared to pledge. I may choose to write my Bid Card number in the box beside the number ninety-nine, meaning I am pledging $99.

This is a great idea that works well when a time limit is imposed (say five minutes), with special recognition going to the quadrant of the room that fills in its flipchart the fastest. The flip sheets with the pledge amounts and Bid Card numbers are then taken to the cashiers for processing.

This is an entertaining way to engage the audience while extracting $5,050. That's how much profit your organization will collect when the one hundred boxes are spoken for.

This is a sample of one of four flipcharts

Pledge $	Bidder #
1	
5	
9	
13	
17	
21	
25	
29	
33	

SPONSORS, TICKETS, UNDERWRITERS, DONORS (STUDS)

CHAPTER 6
SPONSORS, TICKETS, UNDERWRITERS, DONORS (STUDS)

Many organizations fail to recognize the potential for offsetting many, if not all, of their hard costs through sponsorships, ticket sales, underwriters and donors. Let's take a look at how we differentiate each of these.

SPONSORS

Sponsors are corporations or individuals who make a sizable lump-sum cash contribution, usually in exchange for certain benefits at your fundraising event. These funds are normally used at the discretion of the event organizers on an as-needed basis.

For example, ABC Corporation may agree to come on board as a platinum or title sponsor, agreeing to pay a lump sum of $20,000 in exchange for exposure and recognition prior to and during the event. These funds are typically used for covering hard costs.

Companies are often looking at ways to enhance their public image and demonstrate social responsibility, not to mention the fact that charitable giving is an actual line item in many of their budgets. Simply put, most companies have money to give, so why not go after it?

Each sponsorship level carries its own unique recognition package. You should pre-establish different levels of sponsorship prior to approaching potential sponsors.

Here's an example:

▶ **Platinum or Title sponsorship:**   **$20,000 +**

▶ **Gold sponsorship:**   **$10,000 to $19,999**

▶ **Silver sponsorship:**   **$ 5,000 to $ 9,999**

▶ **Bronze sponsorship:**   **$ 1,000 to $ 4,999**

Sponsorship amounts are arbitrary and can be set at the discretion of the event organizer.

Consider seeking item-specific sponsors for such things as:

❑ Parking

❑ Printing

❑ Signage

❑ Printed Program

❑ Cocktail reception

❑ Dinner

❑ Dessert

❑ Wine

❑ Decorations

❑ Centerpieces

❑ Entertainment

❑ Certified Fundraising Auctioneer

❑ Live Auction

❑ Silent Auction

❑ Door prizes

❑ Volunteers

TALKING POINTS

● Item-specific sponsors may not be required to pay the entire cost of the item (dinner or wine, for example) in order to have their name attached to that item. A sponsor may say, "I'll give you $5,000 if I can be recognized as the dinner sponsor," even though the full cost of the meals may be much more than $5,000.

● Gifts-in-kind also confer sponsorship, as in the case where a liquor distributor has provided cases of wine rather than cash. Obviously, this distributor will be your wine sponsor.

The Pitch

Here are a few considerations when pitching potential sponsors:

Do your research—Learn as much as you can about the company you are pitching to. Start by checking their website, and by talking to people who know the company.

Be specific—Proposals need to be specific. Know what you're asking for, and how much the sponsorship item is worth.

Start early—Normally the event should be held at least six months in the future to align with the sponsor's budgeting, and to maximize exposure opportunities for the sponsor.

Connect—It helps if your potential sponsor has an emotional connection to your cause. Company websites and employees can provide valuable insights into the sponsor's community alignment.

Don't over-reach—Be reasonable in your ask.

Write your proposal—Written presentations need to be to-the-point and easy to read. If it makes sense to do so, use point form for such things as features and benefits.

Provide value—Sponsorship of your cause should drive business to the sponsor.

TALKING POINTS

❝ Be aware of possible conflicts, and do not approach a potential sponsor if one of their competitors is already a sponsor.

❝ Sponsors give where they live. Be aware of your potential sponsor's market area or reach.

What Sponsors Want

▶ The main thing sponsors want to know is WIFM—What's in it for me? They want to know how sponsoring your event will drive their business.

▶ Another thing that most sponsors want is the opportunity to work with you in a partnership, and to be able to bring ideas to the table. Invite, and welcome, their input.

▶ They also want to know that you are flexible and will listen to their ideas, and that you will deliver what is promised.

▶ Many sponsors also want to know that this is not a one-time-only opportunity. These sponsors are looking for the possibility of a long-term relationship—make sure you keep the door open to that possibility. Offer your sponsors the opportunity to sponsor other events (golf tournaments, etc.) and keep them engaged throughout the year.

▶ Consider signing a multi-year deal.

The Right People

Competition for sponsorship dollars can be intense, and getting to the right people difficult. Your application must stand out from all of the others. Your request should intrigue a potential sponsor enough that the person in charge of sponsorships wants to meet with you in person.

Warm prospects are easier to pitch than cold ones—who do you know who may know a potential sponsor?

►   Don't dismiss online applications

►   Make your request easy to understand— get right to the point

►   Don't dismiss the 'six degrees of separation' principle

TICKETS

The goal in setting your ticket price is to have ticket sales at least cover your venue and catering costs. Establishing the ticket price then becomes a simple function of dividing these budget expenses by the number of guests expected to attend your event.

Of course, you need to know the number of tickets you must sell to break even.

Here are a few things to consider:

Adding value to the event, perhaps with a better meal, special entertainment, or a celebrity auctioneer, can justify a higher ticket price. Be sure to promote these value-added aspects in your marketing.

Review your ticket price from year to year, and build on past successes. Remember the effects of supply and demand. If your event has generated positive word of mouth and is building momentum from year to year, don't be afraid to bump your ticket price. A $10 increase X 300 tickets = $3,000 in extra revenue. This additional revenue can then be leveraged, perhaps by investing in a professional fundraising auctioneer who, in turn, is going to generate much higher revenues and profits.

Speaking of leverage, try to ensure that tickets to your event are being sold to people who will come and support your cause, not just people coming for a free chicken dinner (as often happens when the boss buys a table to the event but ends up sending employees who have no intention of spending a penny). You're looking for supporters, not chicken-eaters.

TALKING POINT

Some organizations offer a tax receipt for a portion of the ticket price, especially when charging a higher amount for tickets. Typically, the amount of the tax receipt is for the difference between the price of the ticket and the cost of the meal. Check with your tax advisor for accurate information and advice.

UNDERWRITERS

An underwriter is a company or individual who agrees to pay the entire cost for a specific item. This could be the meal, entertainment, printing, professional fundraising auctioneer, or airfare for one of the vacation packages in the auction.

DONORS

Donors are corporations or individuals who give specific items for the auction or for a raffle, or a smaller amount of cash that does not qualify for a sponsorship.

A person or company giving $100, $250, or $500 would be considered a donor, as would somebody giving an item for the Live or Silent auction.

HOT TIP !

When sending invitations to the event, be sure to ask if those unable to attend would still consider making a donation in the amount of the ticket price. You may be able to issue a charitable tax receipt for this type of donation; seek advice from an accountant.

Ask everyone you meet for a donation, be it cash or an auction item. Small amounts of collected money add up quickly, like pocket-change in a coffee can. These funds can then be leveraged. Buy quality items for the Silent Auction or better bottles of wine for the Wine Tree.

CHAPTER 7
CONCLUSION

There is no one-size-fits-all system for creating a successful fundraising auction event. Because of this, combined with the fact that well-intended but inexperienced volunteers organize most charity auctions, results are often hit-and-miss.

I've seen many situations where an auction event has gone well one year and produced excellent results, only to return the next year to witness the wheels falling off the wagon.

How so?

Chances are that a brand new committee of volunteers, working with little more than faded memories of last year's event, has tried to duplicate what may have worked in the past. And now everyone is left shaking their heads and wondering, "What just happened?"

Often, what worked last year isn't going to work this year. Sponsors drift away, donors drop off, and past supporters make other plans. Things change fast.

That said, there are a number of best practices that can—and should—be incorporated into almost every fundraising auction because they're almost guaranteed to bolster your bottom line.

That's the purpose of this book, to share ideas and best practices that will help your organization achieve its full potential and generate record profits at your next fundraising auction event.

As an added bonus, here are sixteen valuable Success Strategies.

SIXTEEN STRATEGIES FOR SUCCESS

Here are sixteen sure-fire strategies that will help generate record profits at your next fundraising auction event:

1. **Invest in quality sound**—It's a sound investment. Nothing will undermine your hard work and ruin your event faster than a bad sound system. Built-in ceiling speakers, the norm in hotel ballrooms and many banquet facilities, do not work for a Live Auction.

   Plan to rent a quality sound system operated by a professional audio technician that incorporates powered speakers in all corners of the room. Trust me, this won't cost you a penny. Quality sound equipment ensures that every guest will be able to hear the speeches, announcements, and auction, thus greatly reducing the likelihood of the emcee and auctioneer losing control of the crowd. We've all seen that happen, with disastrous results.

2. **Develop a plan, and stick to it**—Builders use blueprints, pilots use flight plans, and businesses use business plans, all with an end goal in mind. Does your committee have a goal this year, and a plan in place to achieve it?

3. **Examine what worked in the past, then edit**—Early in the planning stages of any event there should be a serious navel-gazing session. What worked well last year, and what didn't? Be brutally honest.

Even if for the most part things went well, don't be afraid to shake it up a bit and try something new. Incorporate a few fresh ideas every year; your guests will appreciate it.

4. **Consider hiring a professional event planner**—Sometimes it pays to hire a professional event planner, especially if your event is a large one with many moving parts. There are many good reasons to bring in a pro.

Certified event planners have established valuable and reliable relationships with venue operators, caterers, special event rental firms, and other suppliers, and that can translate into enormous savings versus going it on your own.

Another clear benefit is that on the day of your fundraiser the event planner is in charge, leaving key members of your organization free to mix and mingle with guests rather than deal with dozens of last-minute details and distractions.

5. **Go after sponsors, underwriters, and donors**—Many, if not all, of your hard costs can—and should—be offset by sponsorship and underwriting. As well, quality donors help to ensure that you'll have the items needed to raise big money in your Live Auction, Silent Auctions, and Raffles.

6. **Upgrade your auctioneer**—Hiring a professional fundraising auction specialist is not a cost, it's a wise investment. Experience leads to expertise, and that expertise should be made available to your organization well in advance of your event, in the form of creative consultation from your auctioneer.

A Benefit Auctioneer Specialist has been trained to identify and seize opportunities that produce profits. Much as a quarterback is the most important player on a Super Bowl team, so is your Benefit Auctioneer Specialist once the doors have opened. Now the wallets need to be opened.

Think you can't afford to hire a qualified Benefit Auctioneer Specialist? Think again. A top-notch auctioneer isn't going to cost your organization a dime.

7.   Upgrade your Live and Silent auctions— Take a good hard look at your past procurements and see if there's room for improvement. Use my list of 400 Great Auction Items included in this book to stimulate your imagination and spark your brainstorming sessions.

Remember, somebody knows somebody who can flush out those exciting, exceptional auction items. Set your sights high, and don't be afraid to ask.

TALKING POINT

Stick to a maximum of ten to twelve items in your Live Auction and one to 1.5 items per couple in your Silent Auction. If you have too many worthy Live Auction items, peel the extras off and place them in a Super Silent Auction.

8.   Upgrade your audience—One of the most costly mistakes made today is selling corporate tables to your event without expressing your expectations. As a result, the seats are often filled with company employees who have been given free tickets, yet have absolutely no intention of spending a dime at the event to support your cause.

When a company agrees to purchase a table, let it be known that there is an expectation that everybody in attendance is going to contribute. You need spenders at your event, not chicken-eaters. Ask the boss to pass along the message.

As an event organizer, you can help to ensure people participate by including plenty of opportunities in your agenda that engage and entertain every guest while extracting a few of their dollars.

9. ***Issue Bid Card numbers***—Readily available from most auction companies or easily printed by a printing firm, Bid Cards make it easy to track the purchases of your guests. As well, donations offered during a Cash Appeal are quickly captured and easily recorded with Bid Cards.

▶ Using a Bid Card number rather than a name and phone number on a Silent Auction bid sheet ensures privacy for your guests

▶ Because some people don't carry cash, being able to use a Bid Card number to purchase raffle tickets can boost sales

TALKING POINT

Bid cards should measure 8.5 inches X 5.5 inches and be printed on white stock. The numbers should be printed in three-digit number sequences starting with 101. Numbers must be printed in large (300 point), black, bold print and should be underscored to avoid confusion if the card is held upside down.

10. ***Plan to Double-Up***—The fastest and easiest way to drive profits to your bottom line, all Live Auction donors should be asked at the time of procurement if they would consider doubling their donation should a sufficiently high price be achieved.

11. ***Do a dollar round-up***—Have a sign at your checkout asking guests for permission to have their invoice rounded up a few dollars. This can either be a fixed amount (say $20), or a round-up to the nearest $25 or $50. Not much different than adding a gratuity to a restaurant bill.

12. ***Bump your ticket price***—The majority of your guests will barely notice, or even care about, a nominal increase in your ticket price from year to year, especially if it can be demonstrated that improvements have been made and value added to the event (perhaps a better meal, a featured entertainer, a celebrity emcee, or a rock-star auctioneer).

13. *Try a few Walk-away Bid Sheets*—Just for fun, sprinkle a few Walk-away Bid Sheets into your Silent and Super Silent Auction mix. You'll probably be pleasantly surprised at how much some bidders are willing to spend to guarantee they get a certain item.

14. *Incorporate a Cash Appeal*—In their many forms, Cash Appeals can produce outstanding results.

> ## TALKING POINT
>
> ❢ Be prepared to offer charitable tax receipts to donors if your organization qualifies as a registered non-profit, but not before seeking professional advice from your accountant or a tax expert.

15. *Incorporate a Wildcard Auction*—This is a fast and easy way to cast a wide net over the audience to capture extra donations and identify individuals who may become future sponsors and donors.

Look at the Wildcard Auction as 'found money.' If you saw a few thousand dollars lying on the floor, you'd pick it up wouldn't you?

16. *Look for multiple income streams*—In addition to your Live and Silent auctions, look for interesting ways to add additional dollars to your bottom line. Even though his book is full of great ideas for generating extra revenue, the truth is that all the great ideas haven't been thought of yet. So put on your thinking cap and get creative. Have an idea that you think might work? Give it a shot. Just remember the three E's—**Engage, Entertain, and Extract.**

A word of warning—don't overdo the extra revenue generators. People don't want to feel like they're being nickel and dimed.

CHAPTER 8
400 GREAT AUCTION ITEMS

To help you brainstorm, here's a list of 400 ideas for great auction items:

Art

► Authentic Inuit soapstone carvings

► Bronze sculptures

► Chainsaw carvings

► Commission an original painting by a local artist

► Live artwork – a painting or sculpture created by an artist during the auction event

► Oil portrait by a local artist

► Any original artwork

► Children's artwork

Business

► Corporate image makeover – graphic design package that includes logo, letterhead, and business cards

► Business portrait

► Executive office chair

► CEO health & fitness assessment/consultation

► Full page ad in the local paper

► Editorial feature of your company in a business magazine

- Instant investment portfolio of Fortune 500 stock
- Hypnosis Show for your staff party
- Office furniture
- Mentor dinner with a high-profile business leader
- Multimedia advertising package – includes print, radio, and TV
- Naming rights to a street, building, hospital wing or room, etc.
- Outdoor billboard advertising for six months
- Radio advertising package
- Power lunch with an important politician
- Reserved VIP parking space at the office or arena for a year
- Selection of 12 silk neckties from an exclusive Men's Shop
- Travel accessories (suit bag, leather briefcase, Bose headphones, etc.)

Experiences

- After-hours shopping party for the ladies with champagne & hors d'oeurves
- Air combat mission in California
- Airplane ride
- Behind the scenes airport, hospital, or zoo tour
- Behind the scenes tour of…use your imagination!
- Whale watching
- Polar Bear tour to Churchill, MB
- Big Wheel Trucker For a Day – ride along in an 18-wheeler
- Caddy for a day at a pro golf tournament
- Cameo appearance on a TV show or in a movie
- Campout in a teepee
- Co-host a radio Morning Show
- Co-host the 6 o'clock News on TV
- Coach For a Day – shadow a professional sport coach

▶ Concert tickets for a year

▶ Cop For a Day

▶ Day at the gun range for 20

▶ Day at the races

▶ Day in the ER behind the 'No Admittance' doors

▶ Day on a movie set shadowing the director

▶ Day with the Bomb Squad

▶ Day with the K9 Unit

▶ Day with the Police Tactical Unit

▶ Day with a rock band road crew

▶ Big Boy Toy Day – operate various pieces of heavy equipment for a day

▶ Biker Chick For a Day—ride-along on the back of a Harley

▶ Dinner at the Fire Hall hosted by firefighter calendar models

▶ Dinner with a former U.S. President

▶ Dinner with a former Canadian Prime Minister

▶ Dinner with the Premier, Governor, mayor or other local politicians

▶ Discovery flight at a flying school

▶ Extreme driving lessons – race car, police skill course, defensive driving

▶ Farmer for a day – ride a tractor; drive a combine; etc.

▶ Ferrari driving school in Italy (Visit info@italybyferrari.com)

▶ Fireman For a Day

▶ Flying lessons

▶ Guest Ringmaster at the Shrine Circus

▶ Guest conductor at the symphony

▶ Guided hunting experience (wild boar, turkey, bison, predator, gopher, fowl)

- Harvest experience – join a farm family for a day of combining and meals in the field
- Helicopter tour of city at Christmas time
- Hi-tower construction crane operator for a day
- House concert (featuring a recording artist in your home)
- International goodwill mission (to Africa, South America, etc.)
- Irish Pub Party with limo vans
- Jet boating on the river with shore lunch
- Local flight in a fighter jet
- Mario Andretti driving school in Las Vegas
- Winter golf lessons in Arizona or Florida
- Monaco Grand Prix package
- Speaking part on a TV show or in a movie
- Movie passes and restaurant gift certificates for a year
- Observe an open heart surgery
- Pottery lessons
- Ride a float in the parade
- Ride-along in a police helicopter
- Riding lessons (horse, motorcycle, etc.)
- School principal for a day
- Private movie screening for 100 at a local theater
- Private party at a comedy club
- Ride in the Goodyear or MetLife blimp
- Ride in a flight simulator
- Ride in a race car (NASCAR, Indy, Grand Prix)
- Ride in an open cockpit bi-plane
- Ride in a tank and other military vehicles
- Sailing lessons

- Seating for two onstage at the symphony during a live performance
- Soldier for a day
- Sponsor a field trip for a school class
- Table for 8-10 at a major fundraising gala
- Tickets to a TV taping (Dr. Phil, Dr. Oz, Letterman, etc.)
- Tickets to the Academy Awards, Emmy Awards, Grammy Awards
- Tour a diamond mine
- Tour a military base
- Tour an Air Force base
- Tour an aircraft carrier
- Tour a space shuttle launch site with an astronaut
- Tour the Alberta Oil Sands
- Wine tasting hosted by a sommelier
- VIP package for the Calgary Stampede

Food & Wine

- Case(s) of custom-labeled wine
- Catered BBQ for your staff or customers
- Champagne brunch for a group
- Chef's Table dinner in the kitchen of a fine restaurant
- Catered Christmas party at your home or office with a visit from Santa
- Cooking lessons (Thai, Italian, Chinese, Mexican) for a group
- Dinner aboard a restored vintage railcar
- Dinner at the Fire Hall
- Dinner catered by a celebrity chef from the Food Network
- Dinner Club – dinner & wine for four each month a different restaurant

- Dinner with wine for 100 at an Italian restaurant
- Exquisitely decorated cakes
- Fancy Italian espresso machine
- Fine wines displayed on a wine tree
- Fine wine verticals (collections of consecutive vintages e.g. '97, '98, '99, '00, '01, '02)
- Gourmet food & wine baskets
- Greek restaurant party with limo ride
- Hosted dinners (with Police Chief, athletes, celebrities, politicians)
- Lobster feast for a group
- Magnum of fine wine autographed by a celebrity or sport team
- Themed dinner parties (Murder Mystery, clam bakes, pig roasts, etc.)
- Picnic basket full of wine and gourmet goodies
- Private party in an historic building (cabin, house, fort, etc.)
- Progressive dinner (five different courses at five restaurants) with limo service
- Restaurant packages
- Scotch tasting for a group
- Side of AAA beef or bison cut & wrapped for your freezer plus a new BBQ
- Wheelbarrow full of adult beverages
- Wild game dinner
- Wine country tasting tours
- Wine Tree (tiered display of a large wine selection)
- Wine-making lessons and supplies
- VIP table at a gala event (includes beautiful place settings, cutlery, centerpiece, premium wines, table service, bid runners, etc.)

Home & Garden

- Air conditioner or furnace installed in your home or cabin

- Antique furniture
- Appliance package
- Backhoe or Bobcat service
- Backyard makeover
- Backyard custom playground equipment
- Bedroom makeover
- BBQ/Smoker
- Birdhouse/Bird Feeder collection
- Carpentry, plumbing, or handyman services for a day
- Handcrafted cedar Hope Chest
- Handcrafted cedar quilt trunk with a handmade quilt
- Chainsaw
- Collectibles (antique maps, Persian rugs, rare pieces)
- Collection of small kitchen appliances (electric mixer, coffee maker, juicer, etc.)
- Custom shed filled with tools and yard equipment
- Custom furniture pieces
- Custom welded fire pit with swivel cooking grate
- Professionally decorated Christmas tree
- Deluxe custom doghouse
- Dream bedroom suite
- Family portrait session with framed canvas portrait
- Fireproof safe
- Floor lamps
- Framed mirror
- Garden tractor
- Gas powered generator
- Gazebo for the backyard
- Gun safe

- ► Granite countertops
- ► Handmade quilts
- ► Hardwood floors – installed
- ► High end cookware (e.g. All-Clad)
- ► Holiday entertaining package in your home
  (includes decorating, catering, cleanup)
- ► Home entertainment equipment
  (TVs, surround sound systems, etc.)
- ► Home gym package
- ► Home insurance package
- ► Home office makeover
  (furniture, equipment, lighting, office-supply store gift card)
- ► Professional decorating service (Thanksgiving, Christmas, etc.)
- ► Home renovation package (materials and labor)
- ► Home security system installed and monitored
- ► Hot tub – installed
- ► Interior decorating consultation
- ► Interior/exterior house painting
- ► John Deere riding mower
- ► Karaoke machine
- ► Kennel fencing for a dog
- ► Kitchen renovation
- ► Landscape services including spring & fall cleanup
- ► Landscaping package (including hard surfaces and plantings)
- ► Load of dirt or gravel delivered
- ► Log furniture
- ► Luxurious bed linens
- ► Luxury bed & bath makeover
- ► Luxury mattress

- Maid service for a year
- 'Man Cave' – the ultimate garage makeover
- Massage chair
- New patio deck
- Outdoor kitchen
- Outdoor furniture package
- Piano (electric, upright, or Baby Grand)
- Poker table and chairs with poker set
- Pool table
- Portable fire-pit (wood or gas)
- Pottery
- Portable gas patio heater
- Power tools
- Snow blower
- Snow removal for a year
- Stained glass
- Tempur-Pedic® bed
- Tool chest on wheels filled with tools
- Raised vegetable garden custom-built & planted
- Water conditioning equipment – installed
- Water fountain or other water feature – installed
- Wood-burning pizza oven – installed
- Wurlitzer jukebox

Kids

- Basket of Bears – to be distributed at a children's hospital
- Bedtime story read by a celebrity (Robin Williams once donated this!)
- Bedroom makeover (themed)
- Children's concert package and pizza party

- Toy box or dress-up trunk (filled)
- Active Kids' Party (water park, paintball, laser tag, rock climbing)
- Wooden rocking horse
- Disneyland
- Disney Cruise
- Dollhouse
- Elephant ride at the circus
- Hotdog party for grandchild's school class or sport team
- Junior-sized dirt bike or quad
- Kid's playhouse
- Custom-built tree house
- Portable playground set
- Pottery lessons
- Sleepover party at the school, zoo, etc.
- Themed birthday party (Super Hero, Little Princess, etc.)

Leisure

- Acoustic guitar
- Backstage concert passes – Meet 'n Greet with a Star
- Backyard pizza party at a home with a wood-burning pizza oven
- Ballroom dance lessons
- Big screen TV
- Catered dinner in your home
- Complete set of hockey equipment
- Cuban cigars in a humidor
- Custom-fitted golf clubs
- Customized golf cart
- DVD movie collection in basket with popcorn and movie passes

- Golf club membership
- Golf wardrobe makeover
- Electric guitar and amplifier
- Fine jewelry
- Home theater seating
- Home theater system
- Horse saddle & tack
- Houseboat vacation
- Pinball machine
- Recliner easy chair
- Remote control helicopter
- Rolex watches – his and hers
- Shopping sprees
- Spa package
- Stocked beer fridge
- Stocked wine cooler
- Tailgate Party package (includes BBQ, stocked cooler, portable stereo, picnic set, food & drink gift certificates)
- Telescope for star-gazing

Lifestyle

- Acting, music, art, riding, or scuba lessons
- Brand-related items (Harley-Davidson pub table & chairs; John Deere bicycle)
- Crowns for your teeth
- Custom-tailored clothing (shirt, suit, dress)
- Evening with the symphony – meet the conductor (dinner before, dessert after)
- Exercise equipment
- Fitness club membership

▶ Reserved front row seating at midnight Mass on Christmas Eve

▶ Haircuts & color for a year

▶ Harley-Davidson riding gear – full set

▶ His and Hers eyeglasses from an optometry boutique

▶ His and Hers sunglasses

▶ Ladies purses

▶ Luggage set

▶ Louis Vuitton collection (purse, wallet, luggage)

▶ Margarita machine and collection of fine tequilas

▶ Massages for a year

▶ Musical instruments

▶ Music memorabilia

▶ Photo shoot by a celebrity photographer

▶ Sessions with a private fitness trainer

▶ Themed gift baskets (pamper package, spa, gourmet wine & cheese)

▶ Taxi vouchers for those 'nights on the town'

▶ Wardrobe makeover

▶ Western wardrobe (includes hat, shirts, jeans, belt, buckle, & boots)

Recreation

▶ Bowling party for a group

▶ Camping package (tent, sleeping bags, cooler full of beer, camp stove, backpacks, lantern, etc.)

▶ Canoes & kayaks

▶ Family winter sleigh ride and hot chocolate party

▶ Fully equipped fishing boat

▶ Deluxe fly fishing package (rod, reel, creel, vest, waders, lessons, and a guided drift boat trip)

▶ Fully stocked tackle box and new fishing rods & reels

- Golf at 20 different courses
- Golf for three at a private Country Club with a member
- Heli-skiing package
- Mountain biking lessons
- Ocean kayaking trip
- Rock climbing for a group followed by lunch or dinner
- RV rental
- Scrapbooking party
- Ski vacation
- Sky-diving lessons
- Snowboard/ski equipment
- Toys for Boys – (quads, snowmobiles, dirt bikes, etc.)
- Water ski or wakeboard lessons
- Whitewater rafting

Romance

- Breakfast in bed served by a professional caterer on a special occasion
- Dream date-nights for a year
- Flowers for a year
- Glamour or boudoir portrait session – hair, makeup, wardrobe changes
- Helicopter picnic
- Napa Valley getaway
- Romance package at a luxury resort or boutique hotel
- Romantic getaway in a log cabin
- Seaside cottage getaway
- Sunday brunch in a chauffeured Rolls Royce
- Weekend in San Francisco

Sports

► Autographed sport memorabilia (jerseys, helmets, balls, bats, etc.)

► Framed autographed photos of sport legends

► Catered dinner at centre ice in an NHL arena, or centerfield in a football stadium

► Dinner at the Coach's house

► Fly on the professional team charter for a road game

► Join your favorite sports team for a Fly & Golf Getaway

► Game-used hockey stick or baseball bat – autographed

► Hockey school or summer camp

► Premium game tickets with parking passes

► Host your own private golf tournament at a local course

► Locker room tour

► Luxury suites at sporting events

► NFL package with airfare, rooms, and tickets

► Pit passes at the racetrack

► Private ice time at an arena for a season

► Shadow the Coach for a day

► Sport clinic with a pro athlete or coach

► Super Bowl tickets – VIP package

► Tickets to any pro sport championship

► World Junior hockey tickets – VIP package

Technology

► Desktop computer package with printer and accessories

► Laptop computer

► Latest electronic gadgets (tablets, smart phones, etc.)

► Latest smart phone with airtime package

Transportation

- RV (travel trailer, motor home, etc.)
- ATV (quad, side by side, dune buggy, etc.)
- Auto detailing package for all family vehicles
- Bicycles (mountain bikes, vintage-style bikes, etc.)
- Car washes for a year
- Collector car
- Enclosed cargo trailer
- Fiat car
- Fuel for a year
- Four new truck or passenger tires
- Harley-Davidson motorcycle
- Hot air balloon ride
- Limo service
- Year lease on a luxury vehicle
- Weekend rental of luxury vehicle
- Motorcycle with full gear and riding lessons
- Private jet flight
- Vespa scooter
- VIA rail tour
- Windshield replacement

Travel

- African safari
- Bed and Breakfast Getaway
- Covered wagon trek in the Tetons
- Cruise on a private yacht
- Cruise vacation (Caribbean, Mediterranean, Around-the-World)
- Destination special events (Christmas in November at Jasper Park Lodge)

- ▶ Dude ranch getaway
- ▶ Exotic travel destinations – Bali, Turkey, Tahiti
- ▶ Fishing Lodge getaway
- ▶ Golf getaways
- ▶ Kentucky Derby in Lexington, KY
- ▶ Specialty fishing trips
  (fly fishing, west coast salmon, river sturgeon, deep-sea, ice fishing)
- ▶ Girls weekend in New York (shopping, dining, Broadway tickets)
- ▶ Hawaiian vacation
- ▶ VIP trip to the Masters in Augusta
- ▶ Private motor coach for a client or employee appreciation golf getaway
- ▶ Private vacation properties
  (e.g. Villas in Italy, Greece, Hawaii, Mexico)
- ▶ Riverboat cruise
- ▶ Rocky Mountain rail tour
- ▶ Sailboat charter
- ▶ Snooker & Scotch night
- ▶ Staycation – a fun vacation right in your own town
- ▶ Trail ride on horseback in the mountains
- ▶ Travel vouchers
- ▶ Trip to the Olympics
- ▶ Trip to Tuscany (includes villa, cooking lessons, winery tours, etc.)
- ▶ Sun & Sand travel package (includes tanning salon package, luggage, gift certificates to swim shop & sun glass boutique, etc.)
- ▶ Vacation timeshares
- ▶ Weekend in Paris
- ▶ Weekend in Washington with a visit to the Smithsonian Institution
- ▶ Weekend in Vegas

Miscellaneous

▶ First table up to the buffet line, and the chance to pick who goes last!

▶ Autographed guitar signed by a Star

▶ Back cover ad in a sport or concert program

▶ Back cover ad in next year's auction program/catalog

▶ Combine with operator at your farm for a day during harvest

▶ Day of labor donated by a sport team, students, or firefighters

▶ Legacy items
(see Specialty Auctions in Symphony Checklist Builder)

▶ LASIK vision correction surgery

▶ Lotto ticket tree or Treasure Chest filled with lotto tickets

▶ MRI or CAT Scan

▶ Obedience training for a pet

▶ Veterinary services

▶ Mystery purses filled with gift certificates, lotto tickets, and other surprises

SECTION 3

OTHER RESOURCES

SITE ASSESSMENT & VENUE CHECKLIST

Site Assessment

1. SPACE

❏ Is there sufficient space to comfortably accommodate anticipated number of guests plus provide adequate room for Silent Auction tables, Super Silent Auction area, Live Auction displays, bars, registration and cashier tables, etc?

❏ What is the maximum capacity?

❏ Is the space wheelchair accessible?

2. LAYOUT

❏ Does the design of the room lend itself to our requirements?

❏ Are there any obstructed views?

❏ Is there space for large screen PowerPoint and video presentations?

3. EXTRA ROOMS

❏ Are there extra rooms for volunteers, secure storage of auction items, etc?

4. PRODUCTION

❏ Does the venue have suitable sound, lighting, and stage? If not, anticipate extra expenses to rent these items.

❏ Is there adequate power (electrical) to meet the needs of the audio/visual (AV) provider?

5. RESTRICTIONS

❏ Who has control of the thermostat?

❏ Will you have access to lighting controls?

❑ Ask about liquor services and catering (are there kitchen facilities).

❑ Are there restrictions on decorating?

❑ Are there restrictions on access to loading docks or to doors that could impede load-in and load-out?

6. RESTROOMS

❑ Are they easily accessible and adequate?

7. INSURANCE

❑ What coverage does the venue provide and what coverage will you have to provide?

8. WHAT IS INCLUDED IN THE RENTAL FEE?

❑ Tables and chairs

❑ Linens

❑ Staging

❑ Podium

❑ Bars

❑ On-site staff during the event

9. OTHER BOOKINGS

❑ Are there other bookings at the venue at the same time as our event?

❑ Will these compete for parking?

❑ If in an adjacent room, will noise from one event create a disturbance for the other?

❑ Are there any renovations or construction scheduled for the venue at the time of our event?

10. ACCESS

❏ What time can we gain access to the venue for set-up?

❏ Where do we load-in and load-out?

❏ What time must we vacate the venue after the event?

❏ Can any items be left for pickup the next day or following week (if your event is on a Saturday night)?

11. PARKING

❏ Is there free parking?

❏ How far do guests have to walk?

❏ Is there sufficient parking?

❏ Is the parking lot well lit at nighttime?

❏ Is there security in the parking lot?

❏ Will there be snow removal if needed?

TIPS ON BOOKING A VENUE

Consider Placing Your Event Date On Hold

Many venues will allow you to place a 'hold' on their facility for a given period of time. This buys you a little extra time to shop around without feeling pressured into making a commitment and possibly settling for less than you may have found at a venue elsewhere.

Get It In Writing

❑ Make sure all agreements are in writing. A deposit is normally due at the time a rental agreement is signed.

❑ Understand your payment obligations. Be clear on conditions surrounding the deposit.

❑ What is the venue's cancellation policy?

❑ Are gratuities applicable and if so, are they included?

❑ Who is responsible for the liquor license if liquor is being sold or consumed?

Get Contact Info

Make sure you have cell phone numbers for key contacts at the venue in case you have questions or concerns before, during, or after the event.

Rebook Early

Many venues book far in advance, often a year or more. If you've had a successful event and were pleased with the venue, be sure to rebook it for the next year IMMEDIATELY following your event. Consider multi-year bookings if yours is an annual event.

VENUE COMPARISON CHECKLIST

Comparative Site Checklist	1	2	3
General location – is it easy to find and easily accessible?			
Free and sufficient parking? Security? Snow removal if required?			
What is the seating capacity?			
Is there sufficient space in main room for Silent, Super Silent, and Live Auction displays?			
Is there adequate space for Registration & Cashiering?			
Adequate washroom facilities?			
Wheelchair accessible?			
Enough room to set up properly, allowing guests to comfortably and easily navigate the various displays?			
Are sightlines to the stage good from every seat?			
Is there room to set up video screens? Where? What size of screens will fit? What about the projectors?			
Are extra rooms available for secure storage and volunteers?			
Is production (sound, lighting, stage, podium) included? IS IT ADEQUATE? Note: Good sound is CRITICAL!			

Who controls the room lighting and thermostat? Where are controls located?			
Is catering in-house or must it be provided by an off-site vendor?			
Are there adequate kitchen facilities? Health permit in place?			
Will a liquor license be required? Who applies for it?			
Are there decorating restrictions?			
What day/time can we gain access for load-in and setup?			
Is there easy access to loading dock/doors?			
Who supplies insurance?			
Does rental fee include tables, chairs, linens, stage, and podium?			
Does rental fee include any staff (custodian, bartenders, servers, security, etc.)?			
Is there sufficient lighting and space in the registration and cashiering areas?			
Will tables, tablecloths, and chairs be supplied for these areas?			
Is a PDF of the FLOORPLAN available that we can use for planning our layout?			

Will there be other bookings at this venue during our event? Will they create parking/noise issues?			
Are there any renovations or construction planned during our event?			
Can any items (auction, display, etc.) be left onsite for pickup the first business day following our event?			
Will there be a facility supervisor onsite during our event?			
Review Fire Code and emergency procedures/exits			
What time must we vacate the premises?			
Are there cleaning fees? Included in rental fee?			
What is your cancellation policy?			
Is the deposit refundable or non-refundable?			
Are there gratuities? Included in rental fee?			
Can we obtain copy of RENTAL AGREEMENT and place a date on HOLD pending approval of Steering Committee?			
What is your rebooking policy?			

Notes:

LIVE & SILENT AUCTION ACQUISITION FORM

(Insert event logo, name, date, location, mailing address for donations, email, website, contact info, Tax ID or GST Registration #, CATALOG DEADLINE)

Live & Silent Auction Acquisition Form

Donation: _____

_____

Item Tag # _____ ❑ Merchandise ❑ Services ❑ Cash

Fair Market Value: $_____ ❑ LIVE ❑ SILENT ❑ SS AUCTION

Donated by: ❑ Individual ❑ Company ❑ Business card attached?

Name: _____

Address: _____

_____

PC/Zip: _____ email _____ website _____

Contact numbers: T _____ C _____ F _____

Authorized by: _____ Title: _____

Signature: _____

Donation Description (Please list any restrictions): ❑ Actual item ❑ Certificate

_____

_____

_____

_____

If applicable, is donor expecting a tax receipt? ❑ YES ❑ NO

Donation acquired by: _____ T: _____

Is item to be: ❑ DELIVERED ❑ PICKED UP ❑ ACCOMPANYING PROMO MATERIAL

Details: _____

_____

PROCUREMENT LETTER

(On letterhead if possible)

Procurement Letter (SAMPLE)

(Date)

Dear Mr./Mrs./Mss/ (name) (or Supporter):

On (date), (organization) will be hosting a fundraising auction event to benefit (explain the cause) in our community. (Provide details of event). Your support of this important initiative would be greatly appreciated. The purpose of this letter is to request a donation of an auction item that will help us achieve our goal of raising (amount).

Attached is an Auction Acquisition form that you can complete and return by regular mail, fax, or email. Your generosity will be acknowledged in several ways (details). You can be assured the additional visibility for your company will provide a worthwhile benefit to you.

In addition to your donation of an auction item, we are grateful for cash contributions that will go towards underwriting the costs of our event. As well, several levels of sponsorships are available, as are numerous advertising opportunities. An event representative will be happy to explain these options.

On behalf of (organization) and all the other volunteers, I would like to thank you in advance for your consideration of this opportunity to step up and help our community at whatever level and in any capacity you wish. Of course, we would like to invite you to our event, and will gladly add your name to our invitation list so you may be included when our invitations are sent.

Should you require additional information or have any questions, please contact me at any time. My email and telephone numbers are listed below. Again, I thank you for your consideration.

Sincerely,

(Name)
(Title)
(email address)
(Telephone number(s))

AUCTION ACQUISITION SPREADSHEET

Auction Aquisition Spreadsheet (SAMPLE)

#	Item	Description	Tag #	Restrictions	Value	*Assign to	Opening Bid	Min. Raise	Sold for	Donor	Contact	Secured by:
					TOTAL $				TOTAL $			

* **Live, Silent, Super Silent, Raffle, Doorprize (L, S, SS, R, DP)**

NOTE: This is a SAMPLE FORM FOR ILLUSTRATION PURPOSES ONLY - NOT TO SCALE

CASH APPEAL RECORDING FORM

Cash Appeal Recording Form (SAMPLE)

Upon completion of Cash Appeal take this form to Cashier Station

$5,000	$2,500	$1,000	$500	$250	$100	$100	$50	$50
Bidder #	Bidder #	Bidder #	Bidder #	Bidder #	Bidder #	Bidder #	Bidder #	Bidder #
$5,000	$2,500	$1,000	$500	$250	$100	$100	$50	$50
$10,000	$5,000	$2,000	$1,000	$500	$200	$200	$100	$100
$15,000	$7,500	$3,000	$1,500	$750	$300	$300	$150	$150
$20,000	$10,000	$4,000	$2,000	$1,000	$400	$400	$200	$200
$25,000	$12,500	$5,000	$2,500	$1,250	$500	$500	$250	$250
$30,000	$15,000	$6,000	$3,000	$1,500	$600	$600	$300	$300
$35,000	$17,500	$7,000	$3,500	$1,750	$700	$700	$350	$350
$40,000	$20,000	$8,000	$4,000	$2,000	$800	$800	$400	$400
$45,000	$22,500	$9,000	$4,500	$2,250	$900	$900	$450	$450
$50,000	$25,000	$10,000	$5,000	$2,500	$1,000	$1,000	$500	$500
$55,000	$27,500	$11,000	$5,500	$2,750	$1,100	$1,100	$550	$550
$60,000	$30,000	$12,000	$6,000	$3,000	$1,200	$1,200	$600	$600
$65,000	$32,500	$13,000	$6,500	$3,250	$1,300	$1,300	$650	$650
$70,000	$35,000	$14,000	$7,000	$3,500	$1,400	$1,400	$700	$700
$75,000	$37,500	$15,000	$7,500	$3,750	$1,500	$1,500	$750	$750
$80,000	$40,000	$16,000	$8,000	$4,000	$1,600	$1,600	$800	$800
$85,000	$42,500	$17,000	$8,500	$4,250	$1,700	$1,700	$850	$850
$90,000	$45,000	$18,000	$9,000	$4,500	$1,800	$1,800	$900	$900
$95,000	$47,500	$19,000	$9,500	$4,750	$1,900	$1,900	$950	$950
$100,000	$50,000	$20,000	$10,000	$5,000	$2,000	$2,000	$1,000	$1,000
$105,000	$52,500	$21,000	$10,500	$5,250	$2,100	$2,100	$1,050	$1,050
$110,000	$55,000	$22,000	$11,000	$5,500	$2,200	$2,200	$1,100	$1,100
$115,000	$57,500	$23,000	$11,500	$5,750	$2,300	$2,300	$1,150	$1,150
$120,000	$60,000	$24,000	$12,000	$6,000	$2,400	$2,400	$1,200	$1,200
$125,000	$62,500	$25,000	$12,500	$6,250	$2,500	$2,500	$1,250	$1,250
$130,000	$65,000	$26,000	$13,000	$6,500	$2,600	$2,600	$1,300	$1,300
Total	Total	Total	Total	Total	Total	Total	Total	Total

NOTE: Only ONE Bidder number per box

SILENT AUCTION BID SHEET
WITH PRE-PRINTED INCREMENTS

Sample Silent Auction Bid Sheet with Pre-printed Bid Increments ← EVENT NAME/LOGO HERE

COLOR SECTION

Item #	Name of Item

Details in POINT FORM - Description, Restrictions, Donor

VALUE **$500**

BID CARD #	Initials	BID
		$200
		$225
		$250
		$275
		$300
		$325
		$350
		$375
		$400
		$425
		$450
		$475
		$500
		$525
WINNER ✔		$550
		$575
		$600
		$625

Thanks for your support!

SAMPLE BID CARD

Dimensions of the perfect Bid Card - 5.5" X 8.5"
(Print numbers in 300 point font black on white background)

LIVE AUCTION SEQUENCE

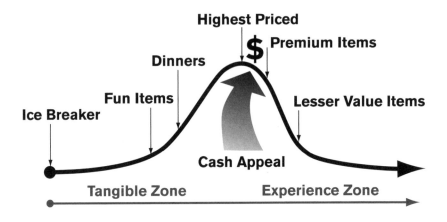

Draw a bell curve and place your most expensive auction items at the top of the curve. Begin the auction with a low-value "ice-breaker," something everyone can bid on.

A common mistake is to save the best (and often most expensive item) for last. In doing this, however, you run a great risk. Suppose that three bidders are holding out for that big trip to Africa, and it is the last auction item. Once the trip sells, what happens to the big bucks those other two bidders were prepared to spend? The auction is now over and they have nothing left to buy.

By clustering your most expensive auction items around the top of the curve, the high-end bidders will still have several large items to bid on after that "marquis" item has sold. The dollar sign ($) indicates the point in the auction at which the Cash Appeal (aka Fund-an-Item, Fund-a-Need, Special Appeal, etc.) should occur. Later than this, and you run the risk that many guests may have already left the event.

WILDCARD RECORDING FORM

WILDCARD AUCTION™

EVENT: _____ DATE: _____

DONOR'S NAME: _____

ADDRESS: _____ CITY: _____

POSTAL CODE: _____ EMAIL: _____

PHONE NUMBERS: _____

COMPANY CONTACT: _____ TITLE: _____

Description of Item / Special Conditions: _____

_____

_____

_____

_____

_____

_____

AIRFARE INCLUDED: ❑ YES   ❑ NO   ❑ N/A

BUYER: _____ BIDDER NUMBER: _____

ADDRESS: _____ CITY: _____

POSTAL CODE: _____ EMAIL: _____

PHONE NUMBERS: _____

PRICE: _____ METHOD OF PAYMENT: ❑ VISA ❑ MC ❑ CHEQUE ❑ CASH

BUYER SIGNATURE: _____

❖ NOT AN OFFICIAL TAX RECEIPT ❖

White - BUYER   Yellow - DONOR   Pink - EVENT   Goldenrod - AUCTIONEER

NOTES:

NOTES:

To contact Danny Hooper visit
www.dannyhooper.com

Follow Danny Hooper Productions on
Facebook and Twitter